SCHOOL, SPORT
and LEISURE

Three dimensions of adolescence

LEO B. HENDRY MSc, MEd, PhD, ABPS
Senior Lecturer in Education, University of Aberdeen

 LEPUS BOOKS • LONDON

© Lepus Books 1978

An associate company of Henry Kimpton Ltd
7 Leighton Place, Leighton Road, London NW5 2QL

ISBN 0 86019 037 4

Typesetting by Malvern Typesetting Services Ltd

Printed in Great Britain at the
University Press, Cambridge

SCHOOL, SPORT AND LEISURE
Three Dimensions of Adolescence

Term time open

Contents

Foreword

The three dimensions which Dr Hendry considers in this book—school, sport and leisure—are seen by many people as sharply contrasting. Sport and leisure are fun activities: school is serious. Sport may be seen by some as competitive and serious, while leisure is considered as purely passive, a non-activity, often a boring process of killing time. School, by contrast, is commonly regarded as compulsory submission to an unwelcome discipline, and the majority of adolescents in this country leave it as soon as they are old enough. Both parents and pupils tend to view school as 'instrumental'—that is, its purpose is to train us for something, for work or perhaps even just to get us through the examinations which stand as a barrier to the type of work we wish to enter—whereas leisure is 'expressive', in that it has no purpose.

Against this background of public attitudes, it is difficult for us to realise that the word 'school' is derived from the Greek word for 'leisure'. Yet much of the present-day curriculum, especially of the secondary school, had its origin as leisure activity. The study of literature, drama, history, music and even science, was originally a luxury of the gentleman of leisure. The luxuries of one age become the necessities of the next: they enter into the culture and the way of life of a community, and the school curriculum must be continually evolving if it is not to be out of touch and out of date.

Can one extend the argument to suggest that possibly some of the activities which are seen as leisure interests of our present day may develop to make a significant contribution to the quality of life of our grandchildren? Sport, for example, promises to become an integral element of the culture of modern society, and insofar as it contributes to personal health and social interaction, it has a considerable potential. If it were to be ignored by our educational institutions, there is a risk that the potential might be lost in mere spectator interest and commercialism.

There is today a strong current of educational opinion which seeks to blur the boundaries of school and leisure, bringing them together in 'community education'. Community schools are being built with facilities for both study and recreation which are shared by school and community. The idea of *l'éducation permanente*, life-long education, is based on the concept of a continuing process which includes adult education and vocational retraining and social and recreational activities, and which cuts across the conventional view that education is an academic concern restricted to the junior members of society.

Freud described adolescence as a period when the individual makes two important adjustments in the transition to adult life, adjustment to sex and adjustment to work. Nowadays we may have to add a third—adjustment to leisure. This is not only because of the shadow of unemployment which hangs over many young school leavers. Leisure is an important part of our lives. For many people, leisure time is the real part of life—when they are most truly themselves, as Aristole said. Yet it is a sad reflection that, for so many, leisure amounts to little more than boredom and loneliness. Is it part of the function of the school to prepare us to use our leisure time more fully and more profitably? If so, we have to admit that the school has not done a very good job. Even physical education, at least in the past, has been singularly unsuccessful in encouraging young people to develop and maintain an active interest in sport.

But the solution does not lie simply in giving more time or attention to physical education or providing better facilities. There are complex attitudinal factors to be taken into account, as is clear if we consider why girls in particular tend to lose interest in sport when they reach adolescence. This is one of the many interesting themes which Dr Hendry discusses, and his analysis not only illuminates the problems but also identifies inherent conflicts which will certainly be difficult to resolve. Thus, for example, there is a 'hidden curriculum' in physical education, a competitive and perhaps aggressively masculine element, which creates conflicts for physical education teachers. Is sport an alternative form of achievement? Is it to be viewed as an alternative form of culture? Or can it be effectively integrated in a liberal view of general education?

The publication of a book which examines the relationship among these three dimensions of adolescence, school, sport and leisure, is therefore timely and important. Dr Hendry's review of previous studies makes this a useful source book, and his account of his own research highlights the issues and establishes a framework for discussion and understanding.

April 1978   John Nisbet

Acknowledgements

I would like to thank the following for permission to include material which has been utilised previously in journal articles:

Scottish Academic Press, Edinburgh and *Scottish Educational Studies*,

Plenum Publishing Company, New York and *Journal of Youth and Adolescence*,

National Foundation for Educational Research, Slough and *Educational Research*, and

Cambridge University Press, London and *British Journal of Social and Clinical Psychology*; also the editors and publishers of

Education in the North (Aberdeen),

International Review of Sports Sociology (Warsaw) and the Chairman of the International Committee for the Sociology of Sport (Cologne).

Further, I wish to acknowledge the considerable help, advice and encouragement given to me, and the tremendous amount of work done for me, by various people in carrying out and presenting a number of research studies which form part of this book: Professor John D. Nisbet and Jennifer Welsh, Department of Education, University of Aberdeen; Professor David Kerridge and Alan J. B. Anderson, Department of Statistics, University of Aberdeen; the co-authors of various journal articles—
Pamela Gillies, Donald Jamie, Fraser McKenzie, Helen Patrick, Alistair Pollitt, David Simpson, David Thornton and Ellis Thorpe; Mr John Blain, Area Physical Education Adviser, Strathclyde Education Authority; the staff and pupils of fifteen comprehensive schools in Central Scotland; and the Scottish Education Department, Edinburgh for a substantial research grant.

L. B. Hendry

Introduction

This book sets out to view school, sport and leisure within the context of adolescence: firstly, by examining previous studies, and secondly, by discussing recent findings of the author from an investigation involving over three thousand fifteen to sixteen year olds during the final two years of their compulsory education in fifteen comprehensive schools. Adolescents' self-identity is considered in the context of school, sport and leisure. Thus these three strands—school, sport, leisure—are explored throughout the text.

Self-identity in adolescence

Elder (1968) argued that at least two-thirds of one's life is characterised by role engagements and by the building of a role repertoire which constitutes a crucial facet of self. The years between childhood and adulthood, for instance, as a period of 'emerging identity', are seen as particularly relevant to the construction of this role repertoire. How, then, is the identity of the individual formed? Several theories have been put forward in recent years of which Erikson's (1968) has been perhaps one of the most influential. According to Erikson, there are eight psychosocial crises extending through one's life-span. Of these crises, most interest has been stirred by his proposal that 'identity formation' is the task of adolescence: 'At this stage of development—between about fifteen and eighteen years of age—the individual tends to be keenly concerned with his self-image. What am I like? How good am I? What should, or might, I become? On what basis shall I judge myself? Many adolescents are consumed with questions of this sort' (Rosenberg, 1965).

The central notion here is that an individual's self develops in relation to the expectations and reactions of other people so that he tends to react to himself as he perceives other people reacting to him. The self, therefore, is seen as a social product, a function of the way in which an individual is reacted to by others. It was Mead (1934) who put forward the theory that self develops when a person begins to take the 'role of the other', that is when an individual takes to himself the attitudes that others take to him. This approach to the study of self-image may be important in the sphere of education. Nash (1973), for example, studied both the effect of teachers' attitudes on pupils as well as the effect of pupil-pupil interaction on children's self-perceptions using the technique of classroom-based observation in combination with Kelly's (1955) repertory grid. Comparatively little attention had been paid to the influence of other pupils—perhaps because the influence of peers in school is not quite so self-evident as the often imposing influence of the teacher. Nash found for instance that certain groups or cliques occurred in the classroom which were 'made up, predominantly, of children either favourably or unfavourably perceived by their teachers'. Additionally, and equally significant, it was found that 'cliques will develop distinct identities which are important in fashioning the self-identities of individuals'.

These ideas about perceptions may be particularly important to the adolescent's self esteem in relation to school, to sports participation, to leisure pursuits, and relations with peers.

School

One of the prime functions of British education has been 'the allocation of life-chances to young people, often in an unequal manner' (Little & Westergaard, 1964; Douglas, 1968). Typically, teachers, pupils and parents define education in terms of 'helping a pupil to get a good job' (Morton-Williams & Finch, 1968; Lindsay, 1969). Thus the social context of education in Britain, and the social organisation of schooling itself, may emphasise élitist values and competition for achievement in wider society. Adherence to such an ideology may not only create educational and social injustice for a large proportion of children but may also be instrumental in preventing educational advance on a broad front (Hoyle, 1969; Midwinter, 1972).

Even non-examinable subjects like physical education do not appear to provide an alternative success system for certain pupils (Start, 1966; Hargreaves, 1967). Emmett (1971), for instance, studied the entire range of leisure pursuits favoured by adolescents in the Manchester conurbation, and emphasised most strongly that many pupils, particularly early leavers, would not continue to have an active involvement in sports on leaving school.

So it can be asked if there are social and psychological influences which affect the aspirations, motivations and self-esteem of different groups of adolescents; and if these factors are consistent in both school and leisure?

Neulinger and Breit (1969, 1971) have argued that attitudes to leisure are basic values, determining in part a person's life-style, and important to the individual's personality—one of the primary functions of leisure being as a source of self-identity. It is possible, therefore, to think of self-identity as reflecting different areas of the individual's life experiences or social roles.

The importance of work as a source of self-identity has also received considerable attention. Argyle (1972) summed up the work situation in these words: 'A person's self image affects his choice of occupation, though . . . the two develop side by side . . . the occupational role and the way it is played is a core feature of identity.' Thus for many people work remains a major source of identity; yet for some individuals leisure may be more important than work as a source of self-identity.

Murdock and Phelps (1973) have argued that the way in which adolescents come to terms with the demands of the school will depend on how they regard their school experience, *and* on their degree of access to alternative cultures. The view of work the adolescent receives from his peer group may lead him to regard work as 'time sold' and leisure as his 'own time'. This could result in school being equated simply with work and attitudes to the two becoming rather similar. That is, education for a large number of pupils may merely be a means to an end, and as representing a contradictory environment to their various leisure styles, and as an inevitable interruption to the 'real' business of living.

Further, since schools are basically concerned with preparing pupils for the world of work, rather than for the world of leisure; preparing for the future rather than seeking fulfilment in the present, then their appeal will be limited to certain pupils. If as Murdock and Phelps have postulated, the underlying values and assumptions of schools are those of the middle class—and these they list as intellectual ability, individual achievement, deference to authority and deferred gratification—then working class pupils will not easily measure up to the teacher's definition of the 'good pupil' role.

As Lacey (1966) and Hargreaves (1967) have pointed out, these factors reinforce the sense of failure of many pupils and lead them to have a low commitment to school as they progress through their secondary education. Murdock & Phelps (1973) have said that 'The emphasis is on cognitive skills and self control, and therefore most forms of emotional and physical expression are either penalized or else carefully regulated and controlled through such devices as school uniforms, supervised games periods . . . (while certain pupils) will be coming to terms with their awakening consciousness of themselves and their physical maturity'.

School and leisure: contradictions? School pupils, like young people in employment, are expected to 'clock in' before nine o'clock in the morning and to perform specified tasks at times determined by their teachers. For a great many the 'work' they do may not be perceived as intrinsically interesting or rewarding.

This contradiction between work and leisure bedevils ideas surrounding 'education for leisure'. It has been suggested by Leigh (1971) that education for leisure attempts 'to increase both the true range of choices available and the ability of the individual to make effective and significant choices.' This is not achieved, however, because the values of work and leisure in society are inter-related. In contrast to the Newsom Report (1963), which implied that leisure can be used as a compensation for boring work, Leigh argued that because of the work-leisure association, education in leisure activities will make dull work less bearable.

Further, it has been postulated that the total structure of secondary education is characterised by contradictions; that is to say, elements in the situation are simultaneously affirmed and negated (Esterton, 1972). In principle, for example, the abolition of selection procedures for secondary education is intended to reduce substantially the operation of social class differentials on educational opportunity. In practice, however, a number of comprehensives operate their own internal sorting procedures, which reconstitute the selective system within the same unit. The resulting gap between promise and practice is often recognised by pupils: 'Because they put on the board "Blank Comprehensive" it doesn't mean it *is* a comprehensive, does it? That's the theory, isn't it, while in practice it ain't.' (Daniel & McGuire, 1972). Within this contradictory setting, the activities which educators often see in terms of the leisure lives of pupils are sports, games, art, music and practical subjects, such as woodwork, metalwork and technical drawing, which even though they may have a vocational bias in a narrow sense, are useful for recreation (Basini, 1975). Often these subjects are additionally offered to pupils in extracurricular time. How do pupils respond to this approach by schools? Do they perceive contradictions in school-based leisure pursuits?

The attempt to resolve the contradictions contained in the school situation through the creation of meaningful styles of leisure frequently takes place within the context provided by a leisure-based subculture. As Murdock and Phelps (1973) pointed out the style of a subculture consists of a particular configuration of symbols and representations, which in the case of adolescents 'typically involve a combination of music, dress, argot, activity and ritual . . . and provide a social and symbolic context for the development and reinforcement of collective identity and in-dividual self esteem. Because subcultures develop to provide solutions to the problems posed by contradictions, and because these contradictions are in turn mediations of the contradictions inherent in the wider class structure, it is scarcely surprising that support for particular subcultures is concentrated among particular class factions.'

Coleman's (1961) study of American schools examined the 'climate of values' of adolescent subcultures, and he found that few leisure activities had any relation to pursuits which go on in school. School may play a less important role in the life of the British adolescent and there is no dominant or elaborate informal social system among pupils. Thus it tends to be the middle class and more academically able pupils who become prefects, members of school clubs and sports teams (e.g. Start, 1966; Hargreaves, 1967; Reid, 1972). In turn, Sugarman (1967) believed that it is pupils who are alienated from school who turn to pop culture—going to discotheques, coffee bars, records, smoking, dating—as an alternative to the pupil role.

Leisure

At a time when leisure facilities are available on a considerable (if not extensive) scale in Britain, it is pertinent to ask how far such leisure proposals represent preconceptions and value-judgements of those who are in positions of influence, since much of what is written about leisure rests on the assumption that certain leisure pursuits are more 'rewarding' and 'worthwhile' than others. In discussing education for leisure Scarlett (1975) stated, 'Hopefully if children are given a model throughout their formative years which is a constructive one, rather than a passive one of merely sitting round the T.V., they will later on seize the opportunities which are available.'

Within Scarlett's (1975) findings on the leisure patterns of Scottish youth, there are points of agreement with Jephcott's (1967) earlier findings. One reason young people in both studies gave for not attending youth groups was that they were too closely linked with school, either because of the pattern of authority and discipline, or because school premises were used. Scarlett also commented on the 'non-constructive' aspects of youngsters' leisure. She argued that working class children were less likely to make 'constructive' use of available leisure opportunities than middle class children, since they have had less encouragement at home to teach them how to use their leisure. It may be that leisure activities are chosen because of different sub-cultural values and life-styles. In common with Jephcott, Scarlett found that a considerable proportion of leisure time was not spent on any definite activity, and that youngsters often announced that they were bored. Many of those who complained of boredom made very little effort in their leisure to take part in any specific activity.

There is little doubt that discotheques and other forms of commercial leisure provision are popular with some sections of young people, possibly due to the independent status such places usually confer on them. If we accept the premise that young people should be allowed to determine for themselves their own leisure provision, it appears that competitive commercial enterprises are only interested in providing for activities with wide profit margins, and to the extent that clubs or coffee bars achieve a virtual monopoly in any area, the young people have to accept what is offered with little opportunity for their own views to be taken into account.

The widely prevalent view that 'sport is good for you' has resulted in an expansion in the provision of sports facilities. This argument is endorsed by Smith (1973) who maintained that the government, in a recent, more positive policy of leisure for youth, 'has generally found it easier to proceed on the firm ground of sport and physical recreation'. The other argument for the provision of sports centres is that they form a vital part of community life. It is claimed that sport and physical recreation are essentially social activities, and that the main attraction for many people is the friendship and companionship found in them (Sports Council, 1968). Indeed, Taylor (1970) predicted that the programme of sports centre development would fail unless ordinary people with little or no sporting skill used these centres frequently, and that if centres became 'expensive clubs for experts', then sooner or later they would have to be closed, as constituting an unjustifiable expenditure of public money. Yet when users in five sports centres were classified into socio-economic groups by occupation, it was found that sixty-eight per cent of all the users were in non-manual occupations and only five per cent came from the unskilled or semi-skilled groups. The remaining twenty-seven per cent were skilled manual workers (Sports Council, 1971). Emmett (1971) has argued that such factors as social class, sex, type of school attended and the teenage subculture generally influence youngsters' behaviour in many ways and affect their view of the world which may, or may not, include certain leisure activities. Emmett's view is that the identity of the adolescent subculture depends on it posing itself against adults, and that 'trendy' adolescents do not participate so much in sport, not only because they are too involved with pop music, dance, dress and so on, but also because adults say that sport is one of the things young people should do with their leisure!

The results from Emmett's study showed that sport and physical recreation may play a less important part in the lives of young people than is often assumed. Sport is only one way a young person can occupy his leisure time and the need for sport does not exist in equal amounts in all young people, and in some, it does not exist at all. The need to meet and form relationships with other young people may be a generally felt need, however, and sport is only one (perhaps not very satisfactory) way of fulfilling this need.

Being liked, accepted, and finding one's identity in a group are important at any age, but may be particularly crucial during adolescence. In interpersonal relations the effect of personal appearance may be crucial. A physically attractive individual is generally believed to possess more favourable personal qualities (e.g. Berscheid & Walster, 1972); he or she is viewed as having greater social power (e.g. Sigall & Aronson, 1969; Sigall, Page & Brown, 1971); and, all other things being equal, physically attractive individuals are liked better than unattractive individuals (Walster, Aronson, Abrahams & Rottman, 1966; Byrne, London & Reeves, 1968). This suggests that physical appearance for both men and women is linked to self-esteem to the extent that it influences feedback from others, which can be either positive or negative (Lerner, 1969, 1969a). Horrocks (1951) was one of the first to point out that a person's physique is to him 'the image of himself'. Reactions to, and expectations of body-type, become incorporated into the recipients own body-concept and 'Thus provide a framework for his body concept, which becomes a significant part of the total self-concept' (Staffieri, 1967).

Further, research has shown that intelligence is positively and significantly related to peer acceptance (Hallworth et al., 1965). Yet it may be that intelligence by itself does not cause either acceptance or rejection. Rather it may be a person's feelings about himself (and others) which are reflected in interpersonal relationships. In this way sport (and attitudes to sport) linked to self-esteem and body image can be seen as a bridging concept between school and leisure in adolescence.

Sport

Discussing the potential development of intellectual ability by 'manipulating the forces that play upon a child as he is growing up', Wolfle (1961) wrote: 'There are three types of factor that can be manipulated: the social climate under which the child is reared; the strength of individual motivation . . . ; and the nature of the educational system.'

Taking Wolfle's quotation in a very broad sense one strand of this book is to examine the 'three types of factor that can be manipulated' in relation to adolescent pupils' involvement in physical activities. By studying individuals who are active in physical activities, and whose degree of involvement can be identified (i.e. competitive or recreative participation), and those who are non-participant, a number of questions can be asked related to their personal make-up, social background, and experiences within the education system.

Emmett (1971) observed that a large percentage of early leavers claimed that they would not continue any kind of physical activity in their post-school leisure. How do such negative attitudes to sports and physical activities develop while adolescents are still at school?

Obviously participation in school sports is related to a variety of personal, social and educational factors. Firstly, with regard to personal influences, 'Below the very highest levels . . . individuals who are thrustful stable extraverts are highly represented' (Hendry, 1970).

The relationship between attitude to sport and ability in physical activities has been shown to be a subtle one, although it is fairly clear that muscularity, for example, *is* associated with selection for the sporting activities (e.g. Tanner, 1964; Watson, 1970). Yet it is virtually impossible for the exercise physiologist to predict who will do well in sporting events from basic laboratory tests—he can do no more than make a crude distinction between athletes and non-athletes.

Secondly, in examining social factors, both Sillitoe (1969) and Emmett (1971) have shown that individuals from a middle class background are more active in physical activities. Emmett (1971) has also demonstrated that adolescent boys are more sports-loving than girls. In this connection, games may be seen as 'miniature achievement models' reflecting particular upbringing, sex roles and life-styles (Sutton-Smith et al., 1963, 1964).

As television looms larger in leisure life, its possible influence should not be forgotten. Himmelweit (1958) found that children in her sample spent more than twice the amount of time watching television than they did on physical recreation. Yet in describing the three main leisure activities they most enjoyed, only girls mentioned televiewing as their first choice more often than sporting pursuits; boys quoted sports involvement twice as often as watching television. Sillitoe (1969) showed that males spent between three and four times as much time on watching television as they did on taking part in physical activities during winter months, and females nine times as much. Wilensky (1964) observed that there was little difference in either time spent on viewing or in the content of what was watched between those who have a college education and those lacking it. There is evidence that this finding holds good for Britain as well as the United States (Blumler & McQuail, 1968). Meyersohn (1968) pointed out that there was no clear-cut, general correlation between the amount of television watched, and the level of participation in other leisure activities, though Emmett (1971) did find differences in the amount of television watched by non-sport-loving adolescents when compared with medium- and high-sport-loving adolescents taken together. This difference held true for both boys and girls. Little is known about why some children find television absorbing and others are uninterested or bored, though Coleman (1961) has argued that children who gain little success within the peer group turn to entertainment with the passive mass media for solace. A recent review found that school pupils' weekly viewing averages varied from thirteen to more than twenty hours, and occasionally reached thirty hours (Murdock & Phelps, 1973).

The third 'manipulative' factor is the educational system itself. Within the educational context the most persuasive influence on sports involvement would appear to be academic stream. Nichols (1971) found a high correlation between attainment in games and mental ability. Previous research in this area has shown similar results (e.g. Start, 1966; Hargreaves, 1967), though this relationship may be the consequence of a complex variety of factors. Reid (1972) has also pointed out that in extracurricular pursuits academically able pupils were over-represented in the prestigious school activities, including physical activities. There have been claims that games within schools (as middle class institutions) reinforce upper academic stream superiority (Hargreaves, 1967), and it is possible to hypothesise that a number of working class families possess value systems which may be counter-productive to the child in his progress through the school. Parental encouragement then must influence involvement in school physical activities.

These ideas may be important in posing a number of questions about adolescent involvement in physical activities in school and leisure. What are the differences between participants and non-participants? What influence does frequent televiewing have on sports participation? More importantly, little is known about which variables are the most powerful influences on sports involvement or about the relationship between school sport and leisure. This led the author and his associates (1975, 1976, 1976a, 1976b) to a preliminary exploration of such questions on samples drawn from university and college of education students, and 'early leavers'. In looking at personal and social factors associated with involvement in physical activities one aspect predominated. The most consistent and significantly associated variable for all samples was what the individual had experienced previously—the background of his or her sports involvement at school. Because sports involvement at school is the key to involvement in leisure or at college or university, it does not necessarily follow that school involvement causes the latter involvement. If certain factors (e.g. physique, personality) are influential in early childhood, perhaps they continue to operate into adult life. Particular characteristics may be a cause of success in physical performance, but there is also the possibility that they are the result of long-term involvement in sport.

At once, therefore, this tells everything and nothing. Such a finding begs consideration of the school situation, the physical education programme, how such personal and social attributes as have been found to be important in previous studies—e.g. physique, social class, personality—affect teacher-pupil perceptions, and the whole range of social interactions from class lessons and school clubs to representative teams, undergone by pupils together with the physical education teacher.

Physical education teachers perceive their main priority lying in social development (Lee, 1968), and the social aspects of the school may become more important as shifts occur within the educational system from a 'closed' to a more 'open' flexible structure (Bernstein, 1967). Additionally, physical education teachers could start off with advantages in terms of reforms, curricular and otherwise, that many fellow teachers may envy. Not only are they free of the restraints imposed by an examination syllabus but they teach a fairly popular subject—or so it would appear (Morton-Williams & Finch, 1968). Sixty-four per cent of boys taking the subject thought it interesting (which puts it well ahead of arts, crafts and music, for example) and fifty-six per cent of girls taking the subject had similar opinions. When asked to rate the subjects studied which they found both interesting and useful—forty-four per cent of boys and thirty per cent of the girls attached this description to physical education, below maths and science for boys, but far ahead of foreign languages and history. As for the girls, eighty-two per cent put housecraft at the top of the list as useful and interesting, forty-four per cent selected maths and thirty per cent saw physical education and games in these terms. These findings are, however, at least eight years old and were before the minimum school leaving age was raised.

There is also some evidence to suggest that in temperament, and by adherence to the expectations of classroom colleagues, the physical education teacher is 'pressed' towards being elitist, aggressive and competitive (Hendry, 1975). Does this mean that physical education teachers play their role in a rather restricted way by concentrating on levels of competitive achievement by few pupils in a limited number of activities? Do these pupils identify closely with physical education teachers and reveal similar competitive, achieving attitudes and drives?

To date little is known of the processes involved in the encounters between the physical education teacher and pupils. It might be asked, for example, what assumptions are made by teachers about pupils according to perceived physical abilities. What assumptions are made about the child's physical status in relation to sex, social class, academic achievement, and peer group status in the school? There is a close relationship between academic stream and representation in school teams (e.g. Start, 1966). But what processes yield this statistically-demonstrated relationship? These questions are important in the light of such findings as those of Emmett (1971) where a large percentage of pupils could mention no sport they thought they would keep up in post-school life. A study of post-school leisure also presented useful insights. After working hours adolescents' leisure life revolved round home, pub, club, dancing, courting and supporting the local football team.

Such ideas should be seen as pieces fitting into a problematic jigsaw puzzle, and the latest perspective has been furnished by the recently completed Schools' Council Enquiry (Kane, 1974). There was a fairly conventional emphasis on topics within physical education: team games, gymnastics, athletics, swimming, dance (for girls) and outdoor pursuits. Teachers considered pupils' interests by gradually lessening compulsion after a fairly restricted programme in the first two years of the secondary school. In their over-all teaching approach to pupils, male teachers favoured direct teaching followed by guided discovery, while for female teachers guided discovery was the most popular style. General teaching objectives were directed towards creating in pupils social awareness and responsibility, self awareness, all round physical development, agility, enjoyment and a general interest in school. Teachers saw themselves as hard working, honest, knowledgeable about pupils and their subject, and with a necessary capacity for sustained hard work. The pupil's view-point remains to be explored in detail, and until there is knowledge of pupils' attitudes and interests the picture remains incomplete.

As Whitfield (1971) noted and questioned: 'How often do we let our pupils as learners into the picture about what is happening to them in terms of changes in behaviour? All too often our curricular intents as teachers are either obscure or remain 'trade secrets'; the curriculum lacks a reality with which the pupil can positively identify himself. In such a situation, we must not be surprised if the pupils rebel, or more tacitly reject much of what we have to offer'. It may be pertinent in relation to physical activities to ask which pupils reject what is offered? At the conclusion of the Schools' Council Survey it was stated that 'It was regretted, for instance, that no children were . . . asked to supply information. Without some knowledge of their attitudes, interests and involvement, one of the main elements which needs to be considered in curriculum planning will be missing' (Kane, 1974).

The suggested dimensions of adolescence—school, sport and leisure—may be inter-related in an extremely complex manner. Attitudes to, and involvement in school, sport and leisure may further reflect these contradictions and differing subcultural values which exist in adolescence. As McIntosh (1963) has commented, 'In sport and dance, human motives are never simple, but it seems justifiable to postulate dominant desires and corresponding satisfactions'. These ideas are explored in the following chapters.

DIMENSION 1
SCHOOL

CHAPTER 1

Pupil self-esteem and peer group popularity

What is known about pupils' self-concepts? How do they see themselves in the school setting? How do they perceive themselves in relation to peers? Esterton (1972) has suggested that contradictions can occur when elements in a situation are simultaneously affirmed *and* negated: in the light of this suggestion Murdock & Phelps (1973) have argued that secondary schools create contradictory situations for many of their pupils. They wrote:

> There is a good deal of evidence to indicate that British secondary schools are in large part reproductions in miniature of the social and ideological universe of the professional and managerial middle class—individual achievement, rational calculation, forward planning and deferment of immediate gratification in favour of long term gains. Yet, the majority of secondary school pupils are from working class homes and are destined for manual employment. *They are thus placed in a contradictory situation, being socialised into assumptions and responses appropriate to a middle class career while at the same time being excluded from the rewards of this system.* The situation facing the middle class 'successes' is somewhat different. . . . As they progress . . . they are expected to consistently improve their level of intellectual performance, while at the same time sublimating their emotional and sexual capacities and channelling their creativity into channels approved by the school. *The contradiction in their situation, therefore, is that the school persistently encourages them to achieve, to 'develop' as individuals, and to 'make the best of themselves', while simultaneously limiting the means through which these ends can be legitimately fulfilled. . . . Due to the very low level of control which pupils possess over the structure of their school situation, these contradictions must be resolved in the sphere of non-work and leisure* [my italics].

Self-esteem and success

A number of studies have shown how various elements of the school system combine to differentiate pupils in terms of their attitude towards school, their friendship groupings, their scholastic success, and their self-images. It is possible, therefore, to consider that adolescent pupils' self concepts in school contain certain reflections of their teachers' expectations. Such an approach to the study of self-image is clearly important in various stages of adolescence. Rosenthal's (1968) study concentrated on identifying the existence of a positive self-fulfilling prophecy by manipulating the teacher's perceptions of pupil ability, while Hargreaves (1967) adopted a much more all-inclusive approach by observing both explicit and implicit attitudes of teachers towards pupils, and vice versa. In the Lumley study (Hargreaves, 1967), teachers favoured pupils of the higher streams who were more conformist to teacher expectations than low stream pupils. It has been shown by Toogood (1967) that the children who are given responsibility by teachers (e.g. made monitors and prefects, given supervisory jobs) are the pupils who are also perceived by the teacher as being more likeable, more co-operative, better behaved, higher attainers. Clearly all this work on the teacher's evaluation and perception of pupils is closely connected with the concept of the self-fulfilling prophecy mentioned above.

By the final year of compulsory schooling many lower-stream pupils have developed a status satisfaction system of their own by establishing what Hargreaves (1967) has called 'a delinquescent subculture', and school experiences have contributed to a greater concentration of pupils into two 'opposing' subcultures. It is also interesting to note the dissatisfactions of low stream pupils with certain aspects of school life as they see it. Richer (1968) realised 'that in the eyes of young people a great deal of contemporary schooling is boring, irrelevant and punitive'. Pupils recognised differences among their teachers and could readily describe good ones as having patience, tolerance and understanding, sharing their pupils' interests and experience, controlling without violence, relaxed, with a sense of humour. But they saw the largest group of teachers as admonitory and domineering, even hostile and rejecting. 'Teachers "treat you like kids", "like infants", "like little ones" right through to the sixth form in some instances. Teachers are portrayed as being coercive, even violently so. Quite apart from the formal system of punishment (which, it should be noted, was rarely criticized and was perhaps generally approved), teachers enforced their will by a whole range of devices, ranging from shouting, blaming, nagging and teasing, "showing you up", "bossing you", and clamping down on rule observance through to a whole range of "rough stuff".' Other common aspects for unfavourable comment were lack of subject choice, morning assembly, 'ridiculous' rules, wearing of uniform and examination goals geared to vocational opportunities.

As Hargreaves (1972) pointed out, it is important to realise that the nature of home and school, together with such others as the influence of peer groups in adolescence and the attitudes and values of the teachers, are mutually reinforcing variables. It can be suggested then that pupil self-esteem in the school context is influenced by the regard in which they are held by their teachers, their perceptions of their scholastic ability in relation to other pupils, their perceptions of teachers and the extent to which their school achievement is supported by their parents.

School values

Despite differing attitudes and viewpoints among pupils, school is universally seen in a strictly instrumental way (e.g. Morton-Williams & Finch, 1968; Lindsay, 1969). Yet such an ideology may create educational and social injustice for a large proportion of children (Hoyle, 1969; Midwinter, 1972). In this way a divisive contradictory school setting may be maintained. Non-academic subjects may also play their part in maintaining this elitist system (McIntosh, 1966; Start, 1966; Hargreaves, 1967). Thus physical education can be a useful instrument of persuasion or coercion; it can aid commitment to school goals and values. At the same time it can be divisive and militate against integrative values at pupil level.

Nevertheless there are symptoms of change. Bernstein (1967) has argued that schools are becoming more 'open' in that there can be a greater recognition of differences among individuals, and with this a weakening of rituals involving shared values, group loyalties, and commitment to school values. One of the essential characteristics of this change would be that school boundaries become more permeable, allowing experience of outside agencies and clearly this will have some bearing on pupils' values. Within this context new mechanisms of value-transmission in schools such as the guidance and counselling system to replace more ritualistic processes such as morning assembly and the house system are functioning. These should be more informal, personal and democratic. (Bernstein et al., 1966).

Thus one cannot presuppose that members of the school system share norms and values in a problem-free manner. Pupils cannot simply be cast as passive recipients of knowledge; there has to be a more realistic notion of conflicting values and interests. Lambert et al. (1973) provide this note of realism in establishing the relationship between the 'formal' and 'informal' social systems in schools. They described the informal system as 'the pattern of norms, values and relationships not prescribed by the official goals of the organization but which still have effects upon these goals'. Yet a number of secondary schools may operate their own internal sorting procedures, which effectively reconstitute a selective system. Thus pupils are caught up in a hierarchical social structure, with little or no power to alter the system. With rewards being given for conformity to and acceptance of the dominant values of the school, 'Schools and colleges remain what they were in origin— secretions of a competitive hierarchical society which trained the mass of its citizenry for low expectations, diligent subordination, and lickspittle admiration of the upper crust' (Council of Europe, 1976). The everyday reality of school life is that of a conservative system which will try to control changes and maintain the status quo. As for the participants in this system; 'The child who achieves well and behaves satisfactorily is bound to please the teacher. [The teacher] in turn, communicates positive feelings towards the child, thus reinforcing his desire to be a good pupil' (Davidson & Lang, 1966).

The link between home and such school values emerges through the behaviour patterns and self images of individual pupils. Brookover and his associates (1965; 1967) argued that the relationship between school success and social class came through the pupil's self-concept. They concluded that self concept of academic ability is a threshold variable. It was suggested that below a certain level of ability children will not succeed in school whatever their social class or self-concept; but if self-concept is low then not even middle class pupils of high ability will do well. Brookover's work suggests that behaviour is under the control of the individual, even though the individual's action may be heavily influenced by background variables such as parental support, or subcultural values and attitudes.

Other aspects of school life may be equally crucial. Hargreaves (1972) has suggested that three variables are important to school success: the teacher's conception of the pupil's ability; the pupil's own conception of his own ability; and whether or not the pupil regards the teacher as a significant other. All these factors have a part to play in bringing about the self-fulfilling prophecy (e.g. Rosenthal, 1968).

Teachers

The reinforcement procedures in acceptance of the school's rules, norms and values on the part of the pupils are 'stage managed' by teachers. As Hargreaves (1967) pointed out, teachers' reactions to pupils are as distinctive and differentiated as individual pupils' attitudes to school. Boys from high academic streams were encouraged and favoured with various privileges; lower stream boys were scarcely tolerated by staff. They were given odd jobs around the school, were the butt of sarcastic comments, and were generally treated ungraciously. Perhaps part of the problem rests in the perceptions of different groups of pupils by teachers—where attitudes are strengthened by the casual comments of the staffroom in everyday meetings among teachers. Given the power differential between teachers and their pupils, society's role expectation is that the teacher should exert authority and thereby impose a 'definition of the situation'. So the pupil's behaviour depends more upon that of the teacher than the reverse. A 'hidden curriculum' exists which each pupil (and to a lesser extent, each teacher) must master if he is to make his way satisfactorily through school (e.g. Jackson, 1968). This means 'learning the system', and pleasing (or ignoring) teacher.

Hallworth (1961, 1962) had teachers rate the personality of their pupils. The results showed that teachers tend to perceive pupils in roughly the same way. In the factor analysis of the ratings, two main factors emerged. The first factor, which was based on the teacher's implicit question 'How does this child get on with me?' was called by Hallworth the factor of conscientiousness and reliability. The second factor seemed to arise from the teacher's implicit question, 'How does this pupil get on with other pupils?' This factor involved such traits as cheerfulness, sense of humour, spontaneity, sociability; it was called by Hallworth the factor of extraversion. These factors were independent of each other; there was relatively little overlap between the first factor—the teacher's pupil—and the second factor—the pupil's pupil. Similar findings come from Nash's (1973) study. In the secondary school, teachers used the dimensions bright-dull, lively-lumpish, likeable-less likeable, well behaved-less well behaved and sociable-less sociable as the central constructs in the typing of pupils. An interesting study by Rust (1970) showed that teachers form a personal typology of what is necessary for pupils' success, then they allow subjective evaluations based on this to influence their professional judgement.

How do pupils perceive teachers? Hargreaves (1972) has indicated that pupils prefer teachers who can keep control, have no favourites and are fair; teachers who explain things, give help where necessary, and give interesting lessons. They like teachers to be cheerful, friendly, patient, understanding, to have a sense of humour, and show interest in pupils as individuals. These perceptions and expectations give rise to implicit rules of conduct for teachers from the pupil's perspective.

School and peers

Jackson (1968) wrote: 'Suppose . . . that a small number of students dislike school intensely and an equally small number are correspondingly positive in their opinion, but that most students have either mixed or very neutral feelings about their classroom experience. Perhaps for attitudes to interact with achievement they have to be extreme, and extreme attitudes, either positive or negative may be much rarer than commonly thought'. Pupils' attitudes towards school may, however, have some influence on friendship choices and in turn these friendships act to strengthen (from the school's viewpoint) positive or negative attitudes. These elements create a complementary reinforcing relationship for pupils, further influenced by subcultural values and school experiences.

Hargreaves' (1967) study of how boys in a streamed secondary school formed friendships clearly showed how these peer groups were sharply differentiated by ability and attitudes towards school. On the whole high academic stream boys were conformist, polite, and well-behaved. By contrast, low stream boys disliked school, intensely disliked some of their teachers and were rude, rebellious and disobedient.

Barker Lunn (1970) has demonstrated that the structure of friendship groups is related to academic ability and social class, while Nash (1973) has also shown that pupil friendship cliques have distinct attitudes towards school, possess their own pattern of behaviour in and out of the classroom, and have their own agreed perceptions of other cliques. Such studies reinforce the proposition that both teachers' evaluations and peers' expectations may be absorbed and integrated into the adolescents' schema of self. More recently, Hargreaves et al. (1975) pointed out a number of constructs or labels which teachers may use in getting to know their pupils. These were: appearance; conformity (or its opposite) to discipline role aspects; conformity (or its opposite) to academic role aspects; likeability; and peer group relations. Two other groups of constructs were also in evidence. The first might be called personality constructs, such as being aggressive, easy-going, extravert, friendly, helpful, shy, self-confident, withdrawn. The second group consisted of a set of highly general 'deviant' labels, such as nuisance, pest, naughty, fool, 'nutcase', trouble-maker, disturbed.

Popularity

It may be that adolescents value qualities in their friendship choices which are different from those necessary for survival and success in the classroom setting. In Parson's (1953) original description of youth culture, two features stood out: its oppositional stance in relation to the adult world and the influence of sex role standards in defining status. Athletic skills, attractiveness to the opposite sex, and a well-rounded 'personality' were important for boys. The 'glamour girl' pattern of sexual attractiveness and popularity was a means for girls to affirm their femininity and gain status. In Parson's description of youth culture, academic excellence had little relevance for peer group status and appeared to be valued or tolerated only if it was accompanied with 'appropriate' sex role qualities. One of the most extreme illustrations of sex role influences on the values of girls was shown in Coleman's (1961) study of the image preferences of girls in a leading crowd; not one wanted to be remembered as a brilliant student. Even today girls acquiesce to pressure thrust upon them to be 'sexy' (Sharpe, 1977).

The extent to which scholarship was viewed by adolescents within the context of manly or womanly characteristics was also shown by a study of adolescent attitudes toward academic excellence (Tannenbaum, 1962). Brilliance was most negatively evaluated as a male characteristic when it was combined with 'bookish' and effeminate characteristics. The potent characteristic was clearly physical prowess. Tannenbaum (1962) noted that 'it doesn't matter whether the student is brilliant or average so long as he is athletic-minded'.

An analysis of the peer ratings made by adolescent girls in a Scottish secondary school (Morrison & Hallworth, 1966) indicated three main 'dimensions' on which peers were perceived and assessed. Furthermore, the results suggested that the perceptions of adolescents are modified considerably both by the age of the raters and by the sex of those rated. When they were rating boys, younger girls gave particular attention to the confidence, appearance and interests of a boy, but the older girls emphasised his maturity, strength, stability and leadership. Also, each age group had its own view on suitability to be a school prefect. For older girls, the boy who was suitable as a prefect was the 'non-academic leader', as defined by leadership, games ability, maturity and strength.

A somewhat different view of youth culture and its effects on academic attainment was presented by Turner (1964). In a sociometric analysis of friendship choices, students nominated as 'brains' were more likely than other students to be chosen as 'friends'. In noting the high status of male and female academic achievers, Turner (1964) tentatively concluded that 'the anti-scholastic values in youth subculture are of ritual character and are at variance with private preference and the determinants of peer-group social prominence'.

Most of these studies emphasise that sex role qualities—particularly athleticism for boys, and attractiveness for girls—are related to peer group popularity. The bedevilling element appears to be academic attainment.

It may be that group popularity allows some children to defy adult rules, and that relative isolation from peers leads other children to seek alliances with adults and to foster this with an acceptance of adults' ideals. However, the crucial matter is that, insofar as popular children are the informal leaders in the school environment, they appear to provide a 'hidden curriculum' for the other pupils that may be in contradiction with the formal system. Peer leaders in their interactions with classmates may be in a position to provide social reinforcement that is both more immediate and of greater reward than that which the teacher can offer.

Pupil self-esteem and popularity. As part of a study by Hendry (1975) involving 3010 pupils the author had pupils describe themselves (i.e. their self concepts) using as many or as few words as they wished. In addition each pupil was asked to list (in order of preference) four or five words describing the qualities which characterised the most popular boys and girls in their classes.

Based on self descriptions a number of recognisable categories or types emerged. There were classified by the author as: 'good', 'neutral', 'disruptive', and 'anxious-mediocre' pupil.
Importantly, academic attainment clearly distinguished among these categories of pupils thus supporting the relationship between school success and pupil self-esteem.

In studying these different categories of pupils, distinctive features were fairly clear-cut and it was because of these distinguishing self ratings that the author felt justified in labelling each type.

What may be particularly interesting about these results is that over half the boys and girls studied apparently abdicated from

Table 1 Classification of pupils' self concepts (Percentages in brackets)

Boys:

'Good pupil' (41%)	'Neutral pupil' (55%)	'Disruptive pupil' (4%)
cheerful good sport good pupil helpful kind popular willing	no distinguishing descriptive words	bossy noisy leader

Girls:

'Good pupil' (32%)	'Neutral pupil' (52%)	'Anxious/mediocre pupil' (16%)
cheerful helpful honest good pupil kind neat polite willing	No distinguishing descriptive words	forgetful helpful honest lazy nervous quiet

describing themselves in discriminating terms in a school context. These pupils belonged to a category for which there were no distinctive terms. This was a miscellaneous group in the sense that it was not obvious what they had in common. It is only possible to suggest that their perceptions of *themselves* in the school setting may have been fairly neutral. Murdock & Phelps (1973) saw school for some children as representing a contradictory environment to various leisure styles centred on 'pop culture'. Taking a less extreme position, in a study of academic success and school satisfaction, Jackson and Lahaderne (1967) found negligible correlations between pupils' satisfaction and scholastic scores. The authors pointed out that 'Perhaps students typically do not either hate school or love it but, instead, feel rather neutral about their classroom experience'. Do Hendry's results in supporting Jackson and Lahaderne's viewpoint then show that feelings of neutrality are becoming more prevalent in school? The current comprehensive high school system of education in Britain may well be instrumental in highlighting and reinforcing such attitudes in pupils. It might be argued that despite a comprehensive ideology many schools effectively reconstitute an internal selective system. The resulting gap between promise and practice is often recognised by pupils (e.g. Daniel & McGuire, 1972) influencing their self perceptions in relation to school, reinforcing conformity or neutrality or antagonism.

The small disruptive group of boys identified themselves as 'leaders', 'noisy', 'bossy' which may merely suggest a tendency to disrupt. Their high extraversion scores further reflected their own self-perceptions. Moreover this potentially 'delinquescent' group revealed high neuroticism scores, which Eysenck (1964) has argued is possibly linked to delinquency. Examining sex differences, Jackson and Getzels (1959) found that boys, in describing their feelings, used 'extrapunitive' adjectives—placing the blame for their condition on others, whereas dissatisfied girls tended to use 'intropunitive' adjectives—placing the blame on themselves. The present typologies (Table 1) might well support such an argument, to the extent that some girls did have a tendency to see themselves in a critical light, blaming themselves for, and rating themselves on, their perceived inadequacies (See Anxious-mediocre pupil).

Turning now to popularity with the peer group this was not found to be associated with cleverness. School-based criteria such as scholastic attainment did not figure as an important quality. While Hargreaves (1972) has argued that there is no overall social system of adolescents in British schools, nor a clear-cut status structure among pupils, it is possible to suggest nevertheless that the underlying hallmarks of adolescent popularity may be consistent and fairly similar in both Britain and America. Typically boys emphasised physical and sexual characteristics of girls. Girls showed a less marked tendency to do this. In boys this clear stress on physical qualities as the main criterion for popularity was matched by a stress on girls' secondary sexual characteristics. Additionally, certain boys assessed a girl's popularity on a purely sexual criterion, described in their own words as 'slack', 'promiscuous', or 'loose'. Yet in choosing some sex peers the choice of qualities, whilst still emphasising physique, laid some greater stress on social relations. (Words such as 'fun to be with', 'sociable', 'considerate', 'sympathetic' were used.)

The number of pupils choosing 'negative' qualities of peer popularity was small, but strikingly there was a comparatively large number of pupils who placed male peers (rather than girls) in this 'negative' category. Thus it is clear that certain pupils saw such qualities as crucial to any description of popular peers. This applied to both boys' and girls' choices. For example, certain popular pupils would be described as 'cheeky', 'fighters', 'hard men', 'show off', 'dough-heads', 'dim', 'stupid', qualities which to an outside observer may not rate as acceptable qualities at all. The point is however that for the few children who used these terms they are, from their persepctive, very positive words!

When pupils use such terms as 'fighters' 'hard men' or 'show-off' as criteria for popularity this may be a possible manifestation of what Hargreaves (1967) called a 'delinquescent subculture'. If pupils truly regard these qualities as grounds for popularity it suggests that non-committed and anti-school groups may be consolidated by labels derived from peer group encounters, and it reflects the reverse side of the labels used by teachers to describe pupils (Hargreaves et al, 1975). That some pupils regard such qualities as good grounds for popularity shows that non-committed and anti-school groups may be developed during the everyday interaction in classroom, playground and street. Academic ability appears to have an impact on certain pupils' self-perceptions, but on the basis of the author's findings the criteria for friendship and popularity among peers for present day adolescents seems as firmly based on valued sex role qualities and centred on the body (i.e. athleticism, physical attractiveness, sexuality) as when Coleman's (1961) and Tannenbaum's (1962) studies were carried out over fifteen years ago.

CHAPTER 2

Raising the school leaving age, academic success and sports

Two recent changes within the British educational system have been the raising of the minimum school leaving age to sixteen years and the reorganisation of secondary schooling along comprehensive lines. Arguments have raged, and still rage, about the academic and social merits of comprehensive schools. Likewise, opinions differ over the raising of the school leaving age (ROSLA). Earlier studies had already outlined differences between those pupils leaving school at the earliest possible opportunity and those voluntarily 'staying on'.

From the results of a large scale investigation Morton-Williams and Finch (1968) painted a general picture of the contrasting qualities of 'early leavers' and the pupils staying on beyond the minimum leaving age:

> It can be seen that 15-year old leavers differed most of all from those staying on at school in the quality of their home backgrounds, which were much less favourable for leavers; in being very much less inclined to have any intellectual or academic interests; and in being . . . more interested in practical-constructional activities than were the stayers . . . On the whole they occupied their leisure time less satisfactorily than did the stayers and more easily became bored or gave their parents cause for anxiety. They were more inclined than the stayers to resent school discipline, they were less identified with and interested in school life, they considered their subject curricula less useful and interesting and their behaviour in school was more likely to be considered unsatisfactory by their teachers.

ROSLA

Despite these possible differences between 'early leavers' and pupils who wish to stay on at school with a view to further education, what are pupils' views about various aspects of school life? Do the majority of pupils generally dislike the idea of raising the school leaving age? What do pupils perceive to be the advantages or disadvantages of remaining in school after the age of fifteen? What qualities and characteristics best distinguish between pupils in favour of raising the school leaving age and those who are not in favour?

Carter (1972) has argued that: 'there is this substantial hard core of young people to whom the idea of remaining at school is abhorrent . . . and (this is) based in a sub-culture and a social system which rejects school and all it is presumed to stand for.' What are the reasons for this?

Murdock and Phelps (1973) have stated that secondary schools in mirroring in miniature the social and ideological universe of the professional middle class reproduce the underlying 'middle class' values of achievement, rational calculation, and deferment of immediate gratification. These values, they pointed out, are alien to a large number of pupils: 'the majority of secondary school pupils . . . are destined for manual employment . . . They are thus placed in a contradictory situation being socialised into (particular) assumptions and responses . . . while at the same time being excluded from the rewards of this system.'

Such a contradictory setting may have implicatons for pupils' attitudes to school. Further, it may be possible to suggest that pupils possessing favourable attitudes to school reveal very different qualities and characteristics from pupils possessing less favourable views about school. It has been argued that two factors are importantly related to pupils having a poor attitude to school. These are: coming from a working class rather than a middle class background (e.g. Morton-Williams and Finch, 1968; Smithers et al., 1974); and showing poor school attainment and a general lack of success in school (e.g. Mitchell and Shepherd 1967; Morton-Williams and Finch, 1968). Not all studies have supported such claims, however, and surveying the rather ambiguous findings Jackson (1968), for example, wrote: 'most students have either mixed or very neutral feelings about their classroom experience. Perhaps for attitudes to interact with achievement they have to be extreme, and extreme attitudes . . . may be much rarer than commonly thought.' Nevertheless, pupil views on the value of education is one factor which does appear to unite students, irrespective of their attitudes to school. Teachers, pupils and parents define schooling in terms of 'helping a pupil to get a good job' and Lotwick (1965), found 'a strong desire on the part of *most* pupils to improve their qualifications'. More recently Smithers et al. (1974) have re-emphasised the instrumental view of education which they claimed is a common one amongst all types of pupils.

Such findings suggest that most pupils will consider 'academic' subjects to be of value to their vocational aspirations, though their interest in such subjects may be more problematic.

A study by Duffy (1972) showed an association between the perceived value of subjects and pupils' reported interest. Adolescents claimed greater interest in what they thought was valuable to them and also asked more questions, learned and remembered more about such subjects. The results of a secondary analysis of Morton-Williams and Finch's (1968) study by Robinson (1975) confirmed this association. The other side of the coin was revealed by Ballantyne's (1974) investigation which in keeping with an instrumental view of education indicated that 'practical' school subjects were valued highly in terms of usefulness and interest. Certain academic subjects were, however, seen as having high utility value but being of low interest.

While the instrumental rewards of school are clearly important to pupils, they are also influenced by the social context of schooling—their interactions with teachers, the nor- mative-affective rewards of the school and so on (e.g. Hargreaves 1972; Nash, 1976). Thus, while Morton-Williams and Finch (1968) discovered subjects were rejected 'in terms of their being out of touch with things modern or outside the range of early leavers' interests or the limited sphere of their vocational aspirations', almost half the sample of pupils also mentioned that they were bored because they were getting 'the same thing all the time', with 'teachers going on and on', while a similar number referred to 'not understanding', 'not being any good at subjects', 'not having subjects explained enough'. Further, most demanded to be 'treated less like children and more like adults'. Robinson's (1975) study has drawn further attention to the problem of bored pupils, pointing out their 'general disenchantment with school and lack of interest in all things educational'. He wrote that: 'Bored pupils were less likely to think their teachers took a great deal of interest in them and more thought that the teacher forgot they were growing up'.

Ballantyne (1974) in a study dealing with pupils actually af- fected by the raising of the school leaving age stated that the greatest number of criticisms which pupils freely voiced were concerned with the general ethos of school discipline. So pupils' orientation towards (or away from) school would appear to be a mixture of both 'instrumental' and 'affective' factors.

In order to explore such issues, at the request of the author the fifteen schools involved were classified by one of the senior ad- ministrative staff of the particular District Education Authority as either 'urban (N = 6), 'suburban' (N = 4) or 'new town' (N = 5), the criterion being one of locality. Two schools from each of those categories were chosen at random and it was from those resultant six schools that a sub-sample of 432 pupils were selected using a method of ratio sampling to examine in closer detail than with all 3000 pupils, *their own personal and particular views* on advantages and disadvantages in raising the school leaving age.

Basically, the general findings were that the majority of pupils (59%) considered that there were advantages to be gained by remaining in school after the age of fifteen. The location of schools, however, had a significant effect on the percentage who were in favour of raising the school leaving age: suburban = 70%; new town = 61%; urban = 49%.

Further the pupils in favour of raising the school leaving age were more likely to come from a middle class background, had higher academic attainment, and a more favourable attitude to school than those who were not in favour. Boys in favour of raising the school leaving age generally considered subjects to be more useful and interesting than those who were not in favour. Differences between the two groups of girls centred on subject interest rather than usefulness of subjects.

Considering the sub-sample of over four hundred pupils it could be seen that pupils' perceptions of advantages and disadvantages of staying on at school centred mainly around instrumental reasons (see Table 2) stressing qualifications on the one hand, and working and earning money on the other. Thus pupils' differing views about staying on at school clearly reflected their attitudes to school generally, with anti-R.O.S.L.A. pupils indicating dissatisfaction with many aspects of school life.

Table 2 Pupils' perceptions of the advantages and disadvantages of remaining in school after the age of fifteen years

Advantages	Frequency (%)
Achieve better qualifications (Higher and O level)	52
A better chance of a good job	22
A wider education	18
Disadvantages	
One could be working and earning money	29
No use if one can't sit exams (or if one's job does not demand O levels)	14
Waste of time/rubbish/hate school	18
Fed up/boring/no interest (teachers and subjects)	11
Can't learn any more/don't need to learn more	14

The existence, overall, of some 22 per cent of fourth year pupils in schools who as a result of the raising of the school leaving age did not wish to remain there (and another 20 per cent who were neutral or uncertain about 'the extra year') can quite easily be interpreted as evidence for Carter's (1972) worst fears about the possibilities of increase in disruptive behaviour among puils in school. Yet as Spencer (1972) in his study of adolescents' attitudes showed, the majority of youth do not seek unorthodox ways of leading satisfying lives and are reasonably content to endorse the values of parents and schools. It may be more realistic therefore to accept that pupils (at worst) '. . . do not either hate school or love it, but rather feel neutral about their classroom experience,' (Jackson and Lahaderne, 1967).

For years the number of pupils 'staying on' at school voluntarily has been increasing, and the present finding that the majority of pupils see advantages in remaining at school to the statutory leaving age of sixteen years merely reinforces the idea of adolescents' acceptance of and perceived values in, extending schooling. Their reasons were strongly instrumental, stressing better qualifications, sound education and 'a good job'.

In discussing the attitudes of pupils to schools, however, it is obvious that one must probe deeper than these general favourable claims. Significantly more pupils in suburban schools perceived advantages in remaining in school after the age of fifteen than did their peers in new town and (especially) in urban schools. It may be more valuable, therefore, to look at why certain pupils are negatively disposed towards raising the school leaving age by asking them their opinions on aspects of school life: subjects, teachers, and so forth and about their views on wider society, rather than simply listing their characteristics and qualities (such as, lower social class and poorer academic attainment; even though these are supportive of previous research findings.) From the point of view of examining the opinions of anti-R.O.S.L.A. pupils, of those who did not wish to remain in school after the age of 15 years a substantial number (29%) stated that they would prefer to be at work rather than at school and a smaller percentage indicated that they regarded remaining in school as valueless if they were not given the chance to sit relevant examinations—a finding that ties up with a similar one of Ballantyne (1974). Additionally, pupils who perceived no advantages in raising the school leaving age placed a much higher social value upon 'earning money' and 'starting work as early as possible' than did their peers who valued raising the school leaving age. Thus the orientation of the anti-R.O.S.L.A. pupil might be described as being one towards work; or perhaps more accurately as one away from school. Working can be associated with money and purchasing power, whereas school is seen as irrelevant. The advantages of work are important to these adolescents; they seem more committed to teenage culture because of the importance they place on social and leisure interests such as clothes, fashions, dancing, having a boyfriend/girlfriend, having a good time while young. Sugarman (1967) believed that it was pupils who were alienated from school who turn to leisure activities such as listening to pop records, going to discos and coffee bars, smoking, dating—as an alternative to the pupil role.

Carter (1972) has sketched in some of the characteristics of the first few years of employment as experienced by the secondary boy and girl. From these studies he stated that the amount of job changing is very substantial. The Crowther Committee (1959) also revealed that as many as 26 per cent of a sample of secondary modern school children had four or more jobs in their first three years after leaving school.

Since it is not the particular job he is going to that specially attracts the pupil, Carter (1972) suggested that what is regarded as a 'vocational impulse' amounts to 'no more than their wish to leave school as soon as possible, to put class-room and teacher behind them and to assume the adult status which they see as properly theirs—a status which the requirement to attend school, where they are treated like kids—denied them'.

Thus it can be suggested that anti-R.O.S.L.A. pupils are motivated as much by a desire to gain adult status within a teenage leisure culture, as by a desire to gain the status of worker. Being a worker may merely provide rewards which can be utilised within the leisure sphere—giving status and enjoyment commensurate with a chosen (and from their perspective, a meaningful) life-style. Raising the school leaving age has merely extended the period of their frustrations and contradictions (cf. Murdock & Phelps, 1973).

Some additional insight may be gained, however, if one examines the views of the pupils regarding those aspects of school life which they complain about. The two most obvious things to look at would be their opinion regarding teachers and subjects. Briefly, the results of the author's study indicated that those pupils who saw no advantages in raising the school leaving age were antipathetic to their teachers and tended to find the subjects which were taught useless, uninteresting and boring.

The typical responses of those pupils who saw no advantages in raising the school leaving age were that they got 'fed up with teachers telling them what they can and can't do'; they did not think that their teachers 'took a great interest in or helped them a lot'; and they considered that their teachers 'forget they are growing up and treat them like kids'.

The causes of this type of pupil/teacher relationship may be manifold, but the point must be made that since the raising of the minimum school leaving age to 16 years, comprehensive schools contain groups of pupils (i.e. pro- and anti-R.O.S.L.A.) with sharply different values, attitudes and aspirations; and in their separate 'instrumental' orientation to work or to school these groups can be compared to Hargreaves' (1967) 'pro-' and 'anti-' school subcultures in a secondary modern school.

If present-day schools do contain (at least) two pupil subcultures, divided along pro- and anti-R.O.S.L.A. lines, with each group exhibiting fairly obvious characteristics (different social backgrounds, academic attainment and so on) then it is possible to ask if these divisions are maintained in the extracurricular life of the school, and even into leisure pursuits? The emphasis in schools in providing what has been called 'worthwhile activities and middle class culture', credentials for careers and society generally, a relatively subject-centred curriculum with early specialisation and a need for long term pupil commitment may produce contradictory elements within the secondary school system which alienates less successful pupils. They experience relative failure in this setting, have a clear awareness of their limited career opportunities and life-chances, feel deluded by the inherent deception of a comprehensive ideology, and therefore turn towards leisure for their self-expression and social existence. Manifestly schools are alienated from, or alienate, such pupils.

Pupil social systems, school success, and sports ability

This can be related back to earlier studies. Hargreaves' (1967) investigation quoted pupils who, because of their negative attitude to school, would not participate in school sports despite having the appropriate skills and abilities. Thus attitudes to raising the minimum school leaving age on the part of school pupils may 'spill over' to other aspects of school such as extracurricular activities, clubs and sports.

Hargreaves (1967) and Lacy (1970) in this country have illustrated the extent of informal pupil systems. Hargreaves' (1967) study of fourth year pupils at a secondary modern school revealed two basic value systems within the school. The academic subculture was characterised by hard work, a high standard of physical hygiene and dress, and avoidance of 'messing about' and causing trouble in class. The delinquescent subculture formed the exact opposite.

Lacey (1970) in a similar type of study, though in a grammar school, found very much the same processes at work. He described the way in which polarization occurs within the pupil body so that school dominated normative values came to be opposed by what he termed the 'anti-group' culture. This particular culture has its attractions firmly fixed outside school, a point which is reinforced by Sugarman (1967) who also saw the focus of teenage social systems as lying clearly outside the school.

Many pupils do not identify with their school, and if physical education is clearly seen by pupils as an integral part of the formal school system, then sports participation will tend to be associated with other kinds of school success. On the other hand, if physical education is perceived by pupils as popular, and different, from academic subjects, it could act as an alternative success area for some pupils within the school. This dichotomy presents something of a dilemma for the physical education teacher. If he goes along with dominant and formal school values he may fail to establish good relationships with the majority of pupils. If he takes a social and affiliative attitude he may not be accepted as a serious and important member of the school staff. Many physical education teachers resolve this conflict by stressing achievement and competitive success. These ideas suggest that physical activities in school can have both a manifest and latent function.

Manifest functions are defined as 'those objective consequences contributing to the adjustment or adaptation of a social system which are intended and recognised by participants in the system'; latent functions 'being those [objective consequences] which are neither intended nor recognised' (Merton, 1949). The popularity of games and sports is not universal, but there are strong indications that abilities such as physical prowess and skill at games form important features of the pupil and teenage value system (Copeland, 1972; Sugarman, 1967). There is further evidence of the part played by physical education in schools and its possible latent functions. Interest at an empirical level has centred on how participation in school physical activities is influenced by peer group (Start, 1963), social class (Eggleston, 1965), and academic streaming (McIntosh, 1966; Start, 1966; Hargreaves, 1967).

McIntosh (1966) argued that success in team games which require tactical skill is more likely to be associated with mental ability than success in individual sports such as track and field athletics and swimming. His findings suggested that in competitive sport as a whole membership of higher ability groups was associated with an enhanced probability of selection for a school team and membership of lower ability groups with a decreased probability of selection. The probability was even less in team games than in certain individual sports involving cardio-vascular response. He concluded: 'It is reasonable to assume that boys and girls who do well in verbal tests will acquire physical skills and tactical manoeuvres quickly under verbal instruction. Two further matters suggest themselves for investigation. What characterizes these comparatively few boys and girls of low mental ability who do succeed in sport? And does the same pattern of success and failure appear in non-competitive activities?'.

This idea is supported by evidence about school sport and extracurricular clubs. Reid (1972) for example, pointed out that it was mainly academically able pupils who associated with prestigious extracurricular activities and these were usually sports teams or school choirs. Membership of higher academic ability groups in comprehensive schools is associated with an enhanced probability of representative selection in competitive sports, and membership of lower academic groups with a decreased probability of selection (McIntosh, 1966; Start, 1966).

Start (1961) pointed out that British pupils who play for school teams also tend to accept the 'academic pupil' role so that sports became another manifestation of school culture. Pupils who were in favour of raising the school leaving age were also significantly more often involved in school sport, and in physical recreation pursuits in their leisure time away from school (Hendry, 1975). These contrasting patterns may be seen more clearly and in greater detail in Table 3: pupils' interest in the school's extracurricular programme and in leisure pursuits away from school revealed clear differences in social class, academic ability and attitudes to school.

Physical education teachers and competition

Westwood (1966) and Wilson (1962) both viewed the pupil-teacher relationship as one of inevitable conflict. Yet in view of the high status placed on games ability and athletic prowess within the pupil system, sports potentially offer one of the very few situations when the official goals of the school organization and the pupil system may be in harmony. It can further reinforce its efficacy as an agent of social control in that organized games involve a reward system. Those pupils who are selected for the team enjoy enhanced status amongst their fellow pupils. On the other hand, it raises important questions about those pupils who are excluded or who exclude themselves for selection, since not all pupils necessarily

Table 3 Extracurricular activities and leisure pursuits: general patterns of social class and academic ability

Pupil involvement in extracurricular school clubs

	Sports participation and non-sporting clubs	Non-sporting clubs	Competitive sport	Recreative sport	Non-participants
Social class	Professional	Professional	Middle	Middle-working	Working
Academic Ability	High	Reasonable	Reasonable	Average	Poor
Attitude to school	Positive	Positive	Positive	Moderate	Negative
Examples of non-sporting activities	Music (esp. girls) Chess (esp. boys)	Drama, Films, Debating Society.			
Pupil involvement in leisure pursuits away from school	Badminton, Squash, Golf, Tennis, Reading, T.V.	Outdoor recreation, Reading, T.V.	Team Games, Reading, T.V.	Dancing, Records, T.V.	Records, T.V., Dancing, Drinking, 'Going out with mates'

(From Hendry, 1975)

enjoy the processes involved.

The physical education teacher appears to experience role conflict from a sense of role vulnerability (Grace, 1972). Musgrove and Taylor (1969) have indicated that a hierarchy of subjects exist within schools. They pointed out that teachers of modern languages and sixth form mathematics are accorded very high prestige by the teaching profession. The secondary modern teacher was placed in a lower position, followed by subject specialists, with the physical education teacher ranked lowest of these. It would seem that the physical education teacher, although a specialist in his own right and enjoying the same basic salary as all other certificated teachers in the country, is distinctly aware of this 'marginality' (Hendry 1975a). Since physical education is a 'non-examinable' subject it cannot be evaluated in the same manner as classroom subjects, thus there is every possibility that subjective criteria may be used by the rest of the pedagogy in assessing standards which give the subject its status within the school. Indeed classroom colleagues see any status that does exist coming via games successes (Hendry, 1975a), thus the fortunes of school teams may be paralleled with school examination results. There is a possibility therefore of the physical education teacher identifying with values expressed by classroom colleagues and thus retaining and using games as a vehicle to obtain 'measurable' results and thereby solidify and possibly enhance his status within the school. A number of physical educationists have become critical of the extension of competition: 'Are we as physical educationists aware of the dangers of more and more competitive school games? . . . All too often the success of the physical education teachers (and of their schools) is measured by the performance of the school teams in local and national competition. A cupboard full of hardware stands in a prominent place and is proudly referred to by the headmaster. Often this is a result of a contentration on one game to the detriment of the rest of the physical education programme' (Wooller, 1975). And 'the axiom of winning is important has changed to winning is everything!' (Crawford, 1976). Indeed, research by Manners and Velden (1974) on the professionalization of attitudes by pre-adolescent boys involved in highly competitive games found that over half the sample selected achievement criteria as of most importance rather than competence or enjoyment. Fitzpatrick (1976) noted similar trends: 'There are ten year olds playing for Sunday football teams and already they are obsessed with the need to achieve that great god, the result!'.

Pupils are themselves aware of the teacher concentrating upon the skilled and more able pupils (Hargreaves, 1967; Hendry,

1975b). Indeed Copeland (1972) saw the extension of games competitions within this country as beginning to exhibit many of the distinctive features that Coleman (1961) described in his American study; features which helped to boost the high status of games within the pupil system. Yet it is possible that physical education can ensure an alternative area to the academic system in which the pupil can achieve status and recognition. But one must not forget the findings of Start (1966) and Hargreaves (1967) who in their different ways concluded that games reinforce upper stream superiority, and that games performance is not inversely related to academic performance. In addition, Hendry (1975) has written of the differential attention given to 'star' pupils and the orientation to elitist values of the subject in some schools. Nevertheless, Start (1966) was forced to admit that general conclusions of upper stream superiority need not embrace the individual boy who is academically poor but highly gifted physically, and who may well achieve compensatory status through sporting skill.

If one wishes to secure maximum participation in sport in the adult population as a means of self-realisation it may require among other things, optimum exposure of the individual to the opportunities for self-expression offered by sport. Munrow (1971) suggested that such exposure is best achieved while the population is captive, and that means during the years of compulsory education. He also pointed out that this is a deceptively simple conclusion which presupposed that there are answers available to many questions about pupils' motivation, teachers' attitudes to the subject, the curriculum, physical skills, physical fitness, and post-school leisure. He concluded: 'With so many independent and inter-related variables contributing to the 'equation', school physical education must be a best-fit answer which implies social orientation and continuing growth'. This would necessitate a change of emphasis within the subject to avoid alienation and rejection: 'Team games and group outdoor pursuits become rather less concerned with individual motor excellences and more with the motives, aspirations, feelings, and reactions of individuals and groups. If concern and praise is not limited to a narrow range of motor skills, all can participate with profit' (Whitfield, 1971).

Hence a conflict can be proposed which suggests that school sports, especially in their competitive forms, reinforce certain values of commitment, conformity and dedication which are rewarded by the school. In this way, pupils of relatively high academic ability and/or from a middle class background receive further 'inducements' to support the school's values. At the same time, this same process may alienate a large number of pupils from different backgrounds who do not conform to or are neutral to school's values and rewards. Nevertheless they may value qualities of physical ability and prowess, but without wishing for the social trappings and processes necessarily involved in 'representing the school'.

DIMENSION 2
SPORT

Physical education teachers and the school sports curriculum: conflicts and dilemmas

In the previous dimension it was suggested that a possible link existed between the 'good pupil' role and participation in school sports. Such findings, however, merely provide a partial insight into the reasons why some adolescents play games and sports, and others do not. Thus the overall purpose of this section is to explore some of the more important educational, personal and social factors which distinguish between those adolescents who are active in physical activities and those who are non-participants in sports.

At the conclusion of a cross-cultural study of involvement in, and attitudes towards, physical activity, Kenyon (1968) wrote: 'As a result of a very limited exploration of factors associated with involvement in sport and physical activity, it was found that a variety of behavioural, dispositional and situational variables were significantly related to . . . different forms of involvement. Involvement tends to be the result of a rather complex set of factors . . . Greater success in the exploration of involvement awaits further research based upon a more definitive theory of involvement and involvement socialization'. Clearly the relationship pattern of various factors to the adolescent's involvement in physical activities is not a simple one. Further, a Scandinavian study has shown how pupils' interests and involvement in physical activities were bound up with their teachers' preferences and influences (Heinila, 1964); and Heinila's findings raise interesting questions about teaching approaches to physical education, about the range of activities offered·to pupils, and about the outcome of such curricular programmes. What is clear from this investigation is that many aspects of the individual pupils' self (the physical self, self-esteem and so on) interact in a complex way with school experiences and social encounters, and the result is that some adolescents get involved in school sports, while many do not.

Prescriptive aims of physical education

Attempts to define the objectives of physical education, accepting it as part of education as a whole rather than as a separate discipline, have been made. The Schools' Council paper (1968) presented the view that physical education was concerned with the balanced growth of each individual by developing physical resources, advancing the skilled and efficient use of these resources, the development of a capacity for creative and imaginative work, assisting the development of initiative, moral and social attitudes, and responsible behaviour, providing purposeful and enjoyable experiences in a sufficient range of activities, encouraging increased responsibility in a choice of activities in school, and providing a sense of achievement and positive attitudes towards participation in post-school physical recreation. More recently (1972) a Working Party of the Scottish Education Department stated: 'The aim of physical education could be said to be that of providing young people with opportunities for activities which have intrinsic value in terms of the health and development of the total personality. Some of its contributions are readily recognised, others less so. It is not always recognised, for instance, that physical education assists the social development of individuals'.

The idea of social and interpersonal relations (synnoetics) has, in fact, been discussed at length by educationists. There is concern in this realm chiefly with the development of understanding between persons, so that the individual may be enabled to see himself in a less egocentric and self-referential manner. Whitfield (1971) wrote: 'If physical education is to contribute significantly to the synnoetic realm in addition to promoting bodily health, a change of emphasis from the acquisition of particular physical skills to an understanding of others in the context of play and leisure is required . . . Then physical education can enable pupils to relax and be relatively free from the unavoidable constraints of other disciplines; a sincerity of relational response becomes more likely'. Such social education within the physical education programme would not detract from aims concerning post-school life: 'Physical education . . . should have helped pupils both indirectly and directly in that they will have a good attitude to physical activity and will have had an introduction to the kind of sports they may pursue as young adults' (Scottish Education Department, 1972).

If prescriptions about physical education recommend that this subject has educational potential in developing social awareness and interpersonal understanding, as well as interesting pupils in physical activities during their school days and for their current and post-school leisure, do empirical findings about the influence of the physical education curriculum and about the teaching approaches of physical education teachers paint the same rosy picture?

Studies of the physical education curriculum

At the outset it must be admitted that there are not a vast number of empirical studies centred on the physical education curriculum, yet the few existing investigations provide interesting insights into this area, and raise many other questions as yet unanswered.

Whitehead (1969) in an extensive survey of the actual content of work in all the male specialist physical education colleges in Britain and a representative sample of boys' secondary schools, found a fairly limited curriculum in operation despite current trends in educational thought and practice. In brief his findings were that although the layman may consider that great strides have been taken in physical education in recent years, the actual content of schools' programmes has changed little. Although the Board of Education in its syllabus of Physical Training for Schools (1933) as far back as the thirties recommended that schools programmes for outdoor lessons should not be confined to soccer, rugby, cricket, hockey and athletics these activities are still included as the major portion of the time allocated for outdoor work. In addition there is not a large element of choice for boys in secondary schools' physical education programmes. Contrary to general trends of individual experience, exploration and invention male physical education teachers spend only a very small portion of their time teaching educational gymnastics and modern educational dance. At the level of official recommendations it has been stated that 'One of the most striking developments in recent years has been the increase of informal outdoor pursuits offered to young people, through the schools and through youth and sports organisations' (Newsom Report, 1963).

The evidence which is available (e.g. Whitehead, 1969) while not refuting that this tendency exists, suggests that the actual change is slow and partial. Additionally a survey of boarding schools showed that while three or more half-days per week are given over to organised games, badminton, golf, fencing and sailing are very definitely minority activities and fives, shooting, squash and basketball are only rarely engaged in by more than half the pupils of any school. Rugby is by far the most prevalent game in these schools and, of the schools for which the information was available, the majority occupied over three-quarters of the pupils in this game (Kalton, 1966).

Whitehead and Hendry (1976) have further reported that despite the inclusion of more educational gymnastics and modern educational dance than are to be found in boys' schools, girls' secondary school sports programmes are selected from familiar traditional activities. The main difference seemed to be the number of schools which regarded various sports activities as appropriate for either boys or girls. For example, fewer girls were 'required' to run cross-country, play cricket or take part in outdoor activities; and there were obvious exclusions of rugby and soccer from girls' programmes, and netball from boys' programmes. 'Finally it could be said that the content of secondary schools' physical education programmes for boys *and* girls seems not to have changed as radically as many have believed' (Whitehead, 1976).

If the prescriptive aims and aspirations outlined for physical education are realised mainly through a rather conservative and traditional programme, then the teachers' approach to the curriculum becomes crucial in attempting to create interest, enjoyment, favourable attitudes to sport on the part of pupils, and in fostering good interpersonal relationships. What is known of teachers' and pupils' perceptions of the physical education programme in British schools? Teachers' perceptions of objectives, content, methodology and teaching strategies have been investigated in a Schools' Council enquiry (Kane, 1974). There was a fairly conventional emphasis on topics within the subject; team games, gymnastics, athletics, swimming, dance (for girls) and outdoor pursuits. Teachers considered pupils interests by lessening compulsion across the years, after a fairly restricted programme in the first two years of the secondary school.

With regard to pupil effects, there was a strongly held view that enjoyment and satisfaction were the main effects of participation in physical activities. Other highly ranked items referred to release from tension, physical development, self-confidence and skills acquisition.

'Social awareness and responsibility', was described as one of the most important effects of their teaching programme, then 'general physical development', followed by self-awareness, general movement ability, general interest in school, enjoyment in physical activity and cognitive judgement.

It would appear that younger teachers give greater priority to social considerations of their subject than older teachers. Their order of values in terms of pupil-outcomes were directed towards leisure, skills, self-realisation, self-awareness and moral development (in that order).

Total work commitment, the diversity of pupils they were

required to teach and the resources available to them were seen by teachers to be most influential in limiting the effectiveness of their work.

When teachers were asked to consider teacher characteristics the highest ranked items included: ability to gain respect of pupils, ability to communicate ideas, and inspire confidence, honesty, integrity, capacity for sustained hard work and knowledge of subject matter. On identifying these underlying factors they were described as: personal education (an all round professional, cultural, academic education); social concern; rapport and good interpersonal relationships; and general psychological, social and educational knowledge of children. The fifth factor emphasised administrative ability and necessary professional links; and the final factor, 'application', described the teacher's capacity for sustained hard work.

Teaching styles, (though they clearly vary according to the demands of different parts of the programme or according to the intended outcomes), viewed overall, showed sex differences. Women favoured guided discovery, problem solving, then direct methods, while in contrast, men emphasised most highly a direct teaching style. Guided discovery and problem solving, which were moderately well emphasised, occupied second and third rank positions.

Rather similar findings were reported by the author (Hendry, 1975) in a study of all the secondary schools in a designated area of Central Scotland. It is possible to suggest, in the light of these studies, that a common ideology runs through the teaching of physical education in Great Britain. Thus, despite variations in the day-to-day encounters between teachers and pupils, in teaching styles among teachers, and in the general 'ethos' of individual schools, general approaches to the sports curriculum, and outcomes in terms of pupil response may show strong commonalities from school to school. Such general findings raise a number of interesting issues about physical education curricula as they exist in schools.

To what extent do teachers in Britain decide for themselves the curriculum which they teach? The claim is frequently made that the teacher (or the principal teacher, head teacher or 'the school') has greater autonomy in this country than in any other. The teacher himself is seldom heard to claim this: he is only too aware of the constraints which bind him, in particular, the secondary school examination system, the textbooks and resources available, the pressures of conventional beliefs and the expectations of colleagues, parents and employers. The area of physical education, in which there are no examination syllabuses to impose a pattern of teaching, offers an opportunity to examine factors which affect the teachers' practices and the curriculum which they teach. Most head teachers give the physical education staff freedom to organise their own curriculum within the limits of a timetable and certain fixed resources. Yet there are constraints operating also on physical education teachers, arising from their own attitudes and assumptions and from their interpretations of the expectations of others. Hidden factors such as these may apply similarly to academic, examinable subjects. They may also point the way to understanding the reasons why curriculum innovation is generally so slow to develop. The point is summarised by Eggleston (1975), who suggested that we are moving towards a situation where 'teachers are free to assert their own arrangements without hindrance by a dominant ideology'; yet curricula are still 'largely conceived within the existing social system . . . The constraints may seem to come, not so much from curriculum development agencies and examining bodies, but rather from the teacher's own consciousness'. This may be because, in a subject-based school system, new ideas can 'deskill teacher and pupil alike, suppressing acquired competencies' (Stenhouse, 1975), thereby attacking the teacher's concept which is bound up with his subject—his rationale, his control of knowledge and of pupils.

It is possible, therefore, to hypothesise a series of dilemmas or conflicts which confront teachers of physical education in realising their aims operationally and which press them towards conformity of attitude and teaching approach hinted at above. Most head teachers apparently give their physical education staff a great deal of freedom to determine the content and pedagogy of the programme, exactly as Eggleston postulated. The absence of formal examinations is a further reason for the considerable autonomy which these teachers enjoy. Thus teachers' decisions concerning the curriculum may have an important bearing on the dominant values of what are considered 'appropriate', 'significant', and 'worthwhile' physical activities for pupils.

A number of questions based on Eggleston's (1975) framework of teachers' curricular decisions in relation to physical education, can be posed to ask how traditional or innovative is the teachers' approach, and how much are pupils expected to 'experience internalization of official values'? How do pupils respond to teachers' curriculum arrangements? What are the possible conflicting influences on the physical education curriculum in secondary schools? In an attempt to offer certain partial answers to these questions an eighteen month investigation was carried out by the author (Hendry, 1975. See appendix for rationale of the study).

This study involved just over 3000 (87%) 15-16 year old secondary school pupils (as they progressed from third year into their fourth year) in 15 comprehensive schools in Central Scotland, together with 75 physical education teachers. As Hargreaves (1967) wrote: 'The assumption is that . . . fourth year . . . represents a crystallization of the values inculcated by the school, and an end-product of the educative process'. Data were collected by questionnaires and inventories, teachers' ratings and assessments, and by direct measurement, observations and recordings. Pupils were categorised as:

active competitively: and (voluntarily) in physical activities or sports at school, i.e. the pupil was actively involved and represented the school in games, sports, or physical activities;

active recreatively: i.e. the individual took part in physical activities or joined sports clubs extracurricularly for reasons such as enjoyment or health but *not* for representative competition; (Both these groups above covered a wide *range* of overlapping sports and physical activities, and did not represent different *forms* of activity)

non-participant: i.e. the individual had no voluntary extra-curricular involvement in school sports or physical activities.

Participation in school sports can range from individual sports such as golf and swimming, through team activities (e.g. hockey) to outdoor pursuits like canoeing and orienteering. It would have been interesting to study different patterns of participation (i.e. outdoor activity participants; team participants; individual pursuits participants) but on examination the pattern was extremely complex, so that while certain pupils could be clearly categorised as 'outdoor', 'team', or 'individual' participants, the majority of sports participants exhibited cross-involvement (e.g. golf, soccer, canoeing) over the school year. Because of this, a broader sports classification of 'competitive' and 'recreative' participation, and 'non-participation', was used.

The teacher: intention and practice

Like their English counterparts surveyed in the Schools' Council enquiry (Kane, 1974), Scottish teachers' aims were very liberal, and certainly reflected a change from the traditional philosophy of strenuous physical training. They tended to stress such aspects as preparation for leisure; the acquisition of physical skills; self realisation, social and moral development; emotional health and stability (see Table 4).

Table 4 Physical education teachers' rank order of selected objectives and effects of physical education

Objectives	Rank order (out of 9) Men	Women
Preparation for leisure pursuits	1	3
The aquisition of physical skills	2	1
Physical development fitness, strength	3	8 equal
Self-realisation—the capitalisation of each individual's abilities	4	2
Development of desirable standards of behaviour and conduct	5	6
Development of social skills and relationships	6	5
Emotional stability—development of personal control and personal adjustment	7	4

Pupil effects	Rank order (out of 13) Men	Women
Enjoyment in physical activity	1	1
General physical development	2	6
Satisfaction from success in physical education	3	2 equal
General self-confidence	4	7
Understanding and getting along with others	5	2 equal
Release from tensions that develop during the school day	6	4 equal
Wide range interests inside and outside of school	7	4 equal

They also perceived a great deal more than physical development (self and social awareness, enthusiasm for sports, satisfaction and success for all pupils) emerging from their courses as a validation of some of their highly rated objectives. Such changes of emphasis are in line with general shifts towards a more open pedagogy, itself a reflection of a society with less certain standards of belief and behaviour (cf. Bernstein, 1967). Hence Eggleston's position is supported in the sense that teachers' objectives were seen to be liberal, wide-ranging and innovatory by their consideration of pupils' personal interests and social awareness as well as their physical development.

The emphasis within the time-tabled programme followed the rather traditional style reported by Whitehead (1969) and Kane

(1974), yet most school provided a very wide extracurricular programme of games, sports and physical activities (see Table 5). One school offered thirteen activities, and the average number of representative competitive activities offered numbered seven for girls, nine for boys. On the surface, therefore, there was some evidence of innovation, development and a wide range of physical activities apparently offered to pupils: but in fact a limited range of activities was taken up by pupils and there were few sports offered *solely and additionally* for recreative reasons. Thus sports club membership was restricted by over half of the teachers on the basis of ability or by teacher's decision. As a result, extracurricular time is devoted to pupils who chose, or are chosen to attend the provided sports, and is not necessarily devoted to all pupils.

Table 5   *Activity emphasis as rated by teachers (a) in time-tabled sports by time devoted to subjects, and (b) in extra-curricular sports by actual involvement*

School Sports	Games	Gym-nastics	Dance	Swimming	Ath-letics	Out-door pur-suits	All other
Time-tabled activities (rankings)							
Men teachers	1	2	—	3	3	—	4
Women teachers	1	2	3	4	5	—	—
Extra-curricular activities (percent.)							
Men teachers	94	14	3	49	60	34	26
Women teachers	100	26	16	34	50	16	21

Hence, the context of most physical education curricula is rather heavily biased towards selective competitive activities of both team and individual forms, even although potentially there may be a wide sports programme available to pupils.

Physical education teachers were asked to indicate which styles of teaching (from a choice of five) they favoured and how frequently they adopted them (Table 6). The general emphasis on direct teaching may be linked with the competition ability emphasis and the teacher-control to which men teachers in particular were biased in running extracurricular club and activities. Clearly such curricular decisions will have some influence on pupils' attitudes towards and actual involvement in school sports, which are discussed in the next section.

Table 6 Frequency of different styles of teaching physical education

Teaching styles	Men Seldom Used	Often used	Women Seldom used	Often used
Direct (i.e. teacher pre-determines learning)	3	27	1	25
Guided discovery (i.e. teacher sets learning situations)	2	19	1	29
Problem solving (i.e. teacher poses problems)	8	11	1	20
Creative (i.e. pupil selects problem and proposes solutions)	20	5	16	8
Individual programmes (i.e. teacher gears pro-gramme to needs of particular pupils)	23	4	22	2

Table 7 Pupil involvement in extracurricular sports

	Boys (%)	Girls (%)
Competitive	26	16
Recreative	17	15
Non-participant	57	69

The pupils' response to the physical education curriculum

More than half the boys, and more than two-thirds of the girls were non-participants in extracurricular school sports (Table 7).

Many schools apparently place great store on the attainments of individuals and teams representing them in 'athletic' competition, and physical education staff are accorded prestige and status for this (Hendry, 1975a). Indeed inter-school games have been described as 'the equivalent, for the physical education teacher, of examination results' (Thomson, 1968). In this way physical education teachers can be party to a general value-emphasis on competition and achievement in schools.

As with academic subjects, such an approach can create dissatisfaction on the part of some pupils with the general teaching of physical education within the time tabled programme. Seldom did non-participant pupils suggest a dislike of the offered activities, rather they commented upon the restrictions and learning situations which they experienced. Adolescent girls were particularly sensitive to changing into sports clothes which did not enhance their appearance (overweight girls reported this frequently). There was a widespread dissatisfaction with sports experiences associated with cold (wet games field, swimming) and full-scale games played in poor weather conditions where several pupils were not directly involved in the action and became soaked and disinterested.

By far the most frequent comments were directed towards the physical education teacher's decisions about the choice of activities, without any real pupil-understanding of the reasons behind these decisions. This has been termed curricular 'trade secrets' (Whitfield, 1971). Perhaps adolescent pupils need insights into fairly specific aims in sports; lesson situations where groups were formed and teachers appeared to give their concentration and attention to skilful players, where pupils felt there was a lack of practices which would enable them to see personal improvement, and feelings of being ignored or left alone by the teacher with little coaching given to them create disinterest.

The reasons offered by pupils for their unwillingness to attend physical education classes if they were run on a voluntary basis throws light on these processes: non-participant girls particularly were not very attracted to physical education on a voluntary basis. Again, reasons revolved around their perceptions of teachers' decisions, 'inappropriate' clothing, learning little of value, not experiencing personal improvement in their skills level, not receiving sufficient coaching, being 'isolated' while skilled performers were given attention by the teacher.

A desire to improve their physical skills was an aspiration of most pupils, including the majority of non-participants. Pupils suggested that this could be achieved in two main ways—by more time being given for physical education and by receiving more attention from physical education teachers. Fewer active pupils desired more encouragement; maybe they were aware that they already received a fair amount of encouragement from teachers in any case!

If physical education became a voluntary subject most active pupils, and a reasonable number of non-participants, would attend. This reinforces the finding that many pupils are interested in and enjoy physical activities and sports; but it also raises many questions about what 'appropriate' teaching approaches for the subject should be.

Some examples of pupils' comments illustrate their feelings about school sports and physical education teachers. 'Youth clubs are for fun and enjoyment: I enjoy going to be with my friends'. *What about school?* 'It's a waste of time . . . you never get taught anything in fourth year!' *What about school sports and P.E.?* 'You do not get taught right . . . the teacher tells you to play rounders then just goes away because she has no time for pupils.'

'I don't like changing for P.E. lessons.'

'Sometimes boring, sometimes O.K., but it depends on what you're doing.'

'They're approachable O.K., but they've no time for you unless you play for the team.'

'They tell you *exactly* what to do . . . I'd like to choose sometimes.'

'Teachers don't take much interest in individual children . . . they concentrate on the "stars" . . . they leave us to play on our own.'

What about extracurricular sports? 'Teachers pick those who go . . . *I* don't know anyone in school clubs!'

Thus the particular emphasis in selection and competition within school sport produced varying responses from pupils. Those pupils who were interested, involved and successful in sports reflected their teachers' values and viewpoints, in that they were highly enthusiastic about sports, desired to improve their skills, and had a very favourable attitude to physical activities and to physical education teachers. The sports curriculum matched the values these pupils possessed or absorbed.

Almost two-thirds of those who were non-participant (beyond the compulsory time-tabled programme) were aware of greater attention given to the physically active pupils, aware that certain activities carried prestige and status, and expressed a dislike of the teaching procedures involved. Yet many non-participants found the actual sports activities enjoyable and desired to improve their individual competence and skills level, suggesting a rejection of curricular processes and emphases, rather than the activities themselves. As Whitfield (1971) wrote, this may represent a curriculum which 'lacks a reality with which the pupil can positively identify himself'. Pupils' attitudes to extracurricular school sports were further reflected in their leisure patterns (see Chapter 6): girls particularly appeared to be indifferent to sports by mid-adolescence and school influences, including teachers' attitudes to pupils, obviously play their part in this. These rejected pupils are more likely to turn to the mass media and pop culture in their leisure time (Sugarman, 1968).

A series of conflicts. Thus a series of dilemmas, contradictions and conflicts can be suggested at various levels. Firstly, in physical activities and sports there appeared to be some expansion of offerings, yet relatively little taken up by pupils: teachers' aims centred on interest and enjoyment, yet competition, status and winning were sought after. This seems to be a deep-seated conflict in the field of physical education. Teachers obviously experienced a reality gap between their stated aims and operational teaching processes, where the underlying ideology of competitive commitment and achievement as expressed in the implementation of the sports programme clashed with their educational aspirations of satisfaction and success for all pupils and of leisure preparation and education. Hence the inherent interest of pupils in sports activities and their desire for personal improvement of their skills level may be lost in the search for competitive achievement. In Eggleston's terms there are innovatory intentions but a traditional system operating within the physical education curriculum. As Stenhouse (1975) stated: 'I believe that our educational realities seldom conform with our educational intentions'.

Linked to this is a professional dilemma for the teacher of physical education. Teachers were asked to rank the 'ideal' qualities of the successful physical education teacher. The items ranked highest were: knowledge about the subject, ability to win pupils' respect, ability to communicate ideas, capacity to work hard, knowledge of children, a good organiser, and ability to inspire confidence. Yet pupils, whilst considering physical education teachers to be approachable, also saw them as competitive, aggressive and giving greater attention to more highly skilled pupils. While pupils who were involved in school sports stated that physical education teachers gave them confidence and acted as pastoral counsellors, non-participants felt quite the opposite! Here, therefore, is a role conflict of the pupil-centred 'guidance' teacher versus the achievement-orientated coach trying to keep up with the academic Jones's. The idea of the physical education teacher's professional dilemma caused by conflicting expectations for his role from pupils and staffroom colleagues has been previously outlined by Hendry (1975a).

A list of postive and negative influences affecting their work in school was compiled by teachers and ranked in order (see opposite). They clearly considered that freedom within a non-examinable subject to experiment with different teaching approaches was the most important positive factor influencing their work. Such freedom, on the one hand, and perceptions of pupil-hostility to school together with the 'intellectual inferiority' label seen to be

Positive influences	*Negative influences*
Freedom to experiment with different teaching approaches	Timetable/teaching load/clerical duties
Recognition from superiors for worthwhile work.	Considerable proportion of pupils hostile to school.
Adequacy of facilities	'Intellectually inferior' label given to physical education teachers.

given to them by colleagues, on the other hand, were suggestive of another area of conflict in teachers' decisions in relation to their orientation to the curriculum.

Thus given the freedom to plan their teaching approach, should physical education teachers devise a curriculum to match the elitist ideology of classroom colleagues thereby winning their respect and gaining status or attempt to provide a programme of 'sport for all' which might be seen as a paternalistic curriculum for social control, building up 'pupils' motivation to conform'?

Secondly, the present system can lead to a situation where pupils who are active sports participants internalise the 'official values' of competition and achievement in both academic and sporting spheres and receive differential treatment from teachers for this adherence to the dominant ideology in the form of greater attention and verbal reinforcement. They can also gain official social rewards by being given positions of responsibility and minor success roles in the school (such as prefects, team captain) and by being praised at school assemblies for competitive success. Pupils were aware of prestige activities and of differential treatment given to those pupils who represented the school in various forms of competitive sports and pursuits. In this way the relational potential of the subject in developing social understanding, relations and social skills (so often cited as a crucial aim for the subject) is ignored so that pupils receive 'messages' of differential prestige and status with consequent effects on their self-esteem particularly in relation to sports participation in both their present and future leisure. Therefore the second conflict relates to the 'appropriate' teaching orientation to adopt based on teachers' curricular decisions and pupils' responses to this approach.

A third dilemma is apparent. Do teachers attempt to maintain their present competitive orientation and continue to risk a high percentage 'drop out' of pupils from voluntary school sport and physical recreation or change their practical teaching approach to encompass a more general source of success and involvement for all pupils, with the possible loss of commitment and dedication by those pupils who are strongly motivated by competitive sports and their resultant status rewards which reflect the values of wider society? A reputation for success in school sports may provide greater incentives for continued involvement in post-school life. A series of post-school studies have shown that despite an association between school sport and leisure sport and between past and current involvement in sport, there was a pronounced tendency to reduce the extent of participation or stop participation in sport on leaving school, but this tendency was less marked among the group who are competitors in school (see Hendry & Douglass, 1975; Hendry, 1976).

Finally, associated with this, physical education teachers are 'pressed' towards fitting in with the expectations of colleagues and the school generally. Yet there seems to be an expectation that teachers should be capable of innovation without anyone realising just how much help may be required in this enterprise. It is hardly surprising therefore that there is a gap between what is actually happening and what physical education teachers think they are setting out to achieve. In any curriculum change there is a need to involve the teacher in the development of the innovation at all stages, otherwise effective change will not occur.

With regard to physical education Munrow (1972) pointed out that one part of the curriculum cannot change unless the rest of the school concurs: 'Games were never more than the fulcrum of an educational system in which many forces of the lever arm operated in substantially the same direction. The whole system was necessary for full effectiveness'. In this quotation may lie the major and basic conflict: 'Curriculum innovation requires change in the internal organisation of the school', and such a change is in itself 'a major innovation' (Hoyle, 1971). Unless in a changing educational climate there are built-in innovatory motivations and tendencies throughout the system it may be extremely difficult for teachers to shift towards a more assertive curriculum, as Eggleston (1975) proposed, and even more difficult for them to conceive and implement a programme based on their legitimate educational aspirations.

Thus there is evidence to support Heinila's (1964) earlier claims of an association between pupil interest and involvement in sports and teachers' influences and approaches to the subject. Clearly pupils who 'identify' with the physical education teacher, his values, and perhaps the values of the total school system are more likely to be interested in school sports.

These investigations, while presenting insights into the general trends in teachers' curricular decisions, carry certain assumptions within their design and methodology. And it is necessary at the conclusion of the chapter to point to newly emerging styles of examining the teaching of physical education.

A more anthropological and open approach to research in the social sciences has recently developed and been debated (e.g. Young, 1971). In this approach there is an attempt to understand the teachers' own criteria. No attempt is made to attain an 'objective' approach, and the assumption is that the constructs teachers use and the accounts they provide make their actions meaningful from their own subjective position. Within physical education the evaluation of lessons from the teacher's perspective has been largely ignored.

An interesting study by Carroll (1976) attempts to redress this balance and it is worth reporting his findings in some detail. Carroll has pointed out that 'teachers may judge any one lesson on a number of criteria, and use many cues which indicate those criteria'.

The main criteria he outlined were:

1 Attainment: acquisition of skill, learning. Cues were in the actual performance; the quality, standard, improvement and progress, but tended to be subjective assessments of pupils' performances in relation to subjective assessments of the pupils' ability.

2 Teaching: presentation, organization. Cues in teachers' performances.

3 Exercise value: fitness; connections here with discipline. Cues—sweating, tired, 'shattered'.

4 Behaviour of pupils; connection also with discipline. Cues—pupils' actions, noise level, movement, following instructions.

5 Pupil's enjoyment—often a by-product. Cues lay in pupils' reactons and expressions.

6 Effort; cues lay in how much pupils appeared to be trying, work rate.

7 Interest—often referred to as 'casual', and often basic to other criteria in what motivation, enjoyment and learning were seen to stem from interest. Cues: expressions, bringing kit, taking part in extracurricular activities, attitudes, attention.

'Effort was often seen as the main criterion of lesson evaluation because, if a pupil was trying his best, then more could not be expected of him, and if he were not learning or progressing, then it was not the pupil's nor the teacher's fault. Low attainment is acceptable as long as effort is high. Effort, too, can be a means of judging the teachers' own success.

When the pupils' behaviour is good, this is often left implicit, and other criteria become more important, but bad behaviour (for whatever reasons) becomes more noticeable and often features as a main criterion in a poor lesson' (Carroll, 1976).

Some additional support for Carroll's framework about the range and subjective basis of teachers' constructs in assessing lessons comes from a recent study by Hendry and Aggleton (1977). They discovered that a total group of final year physical education students attending a specialist college and about to enter their chosen profession exhibited a wide spread of differentiated teaching styles and of criteria used in describing their lesson planning, curriculum organisation and lesson evaluation. Such evidence serves to underline the variety of teaching styles and approaches to physical education engaged in by individual teachers and schools, which nevertheless seem to mask a fairly general ideology of commitment and competition. This in turn may interact with particular qualities and characteristics in individual pupils to produce interest and involvement on the one hand, disillusionment and disinterest on the other. These distinguishing qualities are discussed in the next chapter.

CHAPTER 4

Pupils' and teachers' perceptions: aspects of the hidden curriculum

The qualities and characteristics of individual children in the teaching situation may be important when one considers teachers' expectations of pupils, which can be subsumed under the general term of the Rosenthal effect (Rosenthal & Fode, 1963). There are often personalised factors which interact in a complicated manner to produce teaching bias. One of these factors could well be the child's appearance. A number of recent studies have shown the effect of pupils' physical attractiveness on teachers' expectations and evaluations, (e.g. Dion, 1972; Clifford & Walster, 1973) even when teachers have been made aware of teaching bias (Foster et al., 1975). Thus body build in particular could be a major factor in the teacher's expectanices of pupil performance especially (but not only) in a practical subject such as physical education and sports.

The present chapter explores some of the characteristics which distinguish sports participants, particularly those at the end of their compulsory school careers, and asks if these particular characteristics influence adolescent sports involvement, and the perceptions of pupils and teachers within the context of school sports.

What characteristics have been found to distinguish between sports participants and non-participants? Layman (1972) has provided a useful starting point by stating:

> I think it is clear that play and sports do have potentialities for contributing positively to the attainment of emotional health. On the other hand there are indications that, under some circumstances, with some groups, and for certain individuals sports activities seem unrelated to the development of emotional health or may be detrimental to it. 1 Sports are conducive to emotional health if they promote physical fitness, *but not all sports promote physical fitness*; 2 They encourage healthy emotional development if the participant has enough skill to merit the approval and admiration of his peers, and enough so that he can have a feeling of success, *but not all participants will have such*

skills; 3 They encourage healthy emotional development if the participant can use them for spontaneous expression of positive feelings and discharge of aggressive tensions, *but not all participants have emotional experiences of this type* [my italics].

This suggests that a range of characteristics, beyond that of body type, are evident in sports participants—fitness, skill, psychological traits—and that participation in sports need not necessarily provide a testing ground for sterling qualities or positive experiences for the participant. The evidence relating to these factors is discussed below.

Physique, personality and sports involvement

Most studies have shown that muscular individuals tend to excel in physical ability and performance (e.g. Parnell, 1954, 1958; Tanner, 1964), whereas those with low muscularity or fat tend to be non-athletic types showing little interest in sport (e.g. Willgoose, 1961).

At schoolboy level, for example, Parsons (1973) has suggested the possibility of athletic prediction through the classification of physique. The object of this study was to discover whether there was any relationship between the physique of adolescent boys who had achieved above average performances in either long jump or triple jump, and the physique of international athletes. Results indicated similarities between pupils and athletes, and an identical high rating in muscularity. Watson (1970) in showing the importance of muscularity to selection for representative school rugby wrote 'There are obviously other factors that contribute to the make up of a rugger player besides physique. One of the most important of these is probably personality, rugger is an aggressive game and only a certain type of person is likely to enjoy playing it'. A subjective 'aggression' assessment of pupils was found by Watson to correlate fairly highly ($+0.72$) with their muscularity scores. Clearly evidence points to the importance of muscularity in sports participation. It may be asked, however, if mesomorphy is only crucial to competitive involvement: and if recreational activities in British schools cater for a much wider range of body types?

Personality is another aspect which has merited considerable research particularly from the mid 1960s up till the early 1970s. In an experiment to investigate the relationship of exercise response to personality dimensions, Stanaway and Hullin (1973) found a highly significant positive correlation between neuroticism and physiological changes commensurate with Eysenck's (1967) theory in which neuroticism is conceptualised as a measure of the reactivity of the autonomic nervous sytem to stress. Stable extraverts may be considered as being low in both arousal and arousability which may put them at a disadvantage in mental tasks but may enable them to perform well in physical endurance tasks which capitalise on their low physiological activation. (The way in which arousal affects performance of any kind is complex however, and there appear to be a numer of factors including task difficulty and situational stress affecting the relationship.)

A number of detailed reviews have given a personality description of athletes in terms of extravert tendencies (high dominance, social aggression, tough-mindedness) and general emotional control reflected in such trait measurements as low anxiety (Warburton & Kane, 1967); Ogilvie, 1968; Hendry, 1970b). There are, of course, many exceptions to these general descriptions, and no doubt both the nature of the physical activity in question and the subjects' level of participation will in some way be reflected in findings.

If personality differences are in any way attributable to the 'athletic' environment, then presumably the cause and effect reaction takes place before maturity. On this point Tattersfield (1971) comparing 106 adolescent schoolboys involved in competitive (age-group) swimming with a matched group of pupils who were not competitive, found that over a period of two years (i.e. from 12 to 14 years of age) the competitive group showed more marked personality changes than did the control group in becoming more extraverted, less anxious, and less independent.

Considering the evidence on personality and physical performance in relation to adolescents Whiting & Stembridge (1965) earlier showed that persistent non-swimmers were significantly more neurotic and introverted than swimmers. Further, using a sample of 412 boys of average age 14 years, in secondary schools, Kane's (1962) findings were that extraversion related significantly to competitive skills and general motor ability. Some support for these findings comes from studies by Hardman (1962) and Herbert (1965) who investigated the personality correlates of physical skill among boys between 12 and 15 years. These studies provide a general picture of the physically gifted adolescent boy in personality terms of aggressive extraversion. Herbert and Steel (1968) found that boys who performed best at a physical skill under stress were those high on stability, low on excitability and low on anxiety.

Thus, while it may be an over-simplification, there seems to be a relationship between sporting achievement and emotional stability with extraversion, particularly in adolescence. As I have pointed out elsewhere, 'It is possible that non-intellectual factors may also operate in the area of sporting success. Certainly below the highest levels of sports achievement individuals who are shown to be stable thrustful extraverts are highly represented. The introverted individual, particularly when this personality disposition is associated with a poor physique does not participate in vigorous physical activities, and, therefore, does not gain group status in adolescence . . . Below a certain level of muscularity and extraversion, motivation toward participation is reduced' (Hendry, 1970b).

POMS

With regard to athletic participants of higher calibre and more mature years, however, Kane (1964) and Hardman (1973) have intimated that it is not necessarily an asset to be absolutely well-adapted and thrustful—top level successes may well be anxious and introverted!

In the field of psychology certain basic human types have been proposed in an effort to simplify the observable variations among individuals. Sheldon (1942) proposed three somatotype dimensions, endomorphy (fat), mesomorphy (muscle) and ectomorphy (linearity) which were significantly related to three corresponding temperamental scales, visceratonia (relaxed), somatotonia (energetic) and cerebretonia (detached) as follows: endomorphy and visceratonia $+0.79$; mesomorphy and somatotonia $+0.82$; ectomorphy and cerebretonia $+0.83$. These correlations are higher than any found by other investigators (e.g. Kane, 1969; Hendry, 1970b), and it may be that the relationship between physique and temperament is general rather than specific. Such general measures were used in a study by Sugarman and Haronian (1964), where they found a moderate positive relationship between sophistication-of-body concept and muscularity and a moderate negative association between the body sophistication scores and endomorphy (fat).

They noted: 'Students who are high in mesomorphy are more likely to take part in strenuous physical activity than others. Participation . . . might also have a direct effect on their body image . . . athletic subjects presumably have more defined concepts of their bodies than subjects without athletic experience'.

Further it may be that the development of a positive body concept will depend to some extent on the differential, social and personal approval given to varying body types. On this point, McCandless (1960) wrote, 'The beautiful body serves purposes related to fantasy, displacement, projection and wish fulfillment; heroes of popular novels and in the movies and on the television screen are broad-shouldered, narrow-hipped, possess flat abdomens and are muscular'.

Goffman (1963) has suggested that like the Greeks our society is 'Strong in visual aids'. There are, in more or less clearly defined terms, notions of what is desirable in a person's physical appearance in respect of body type. 'One explanation may be that the personally and socially favourable emphasis which western culture has placed on the mesomorphic body type has resulted in a consistently evoked stereotyped reaction to that body type in terms of a cultural physique ideal' (Dibiase & Hjelle, 1968). These ideals are transmitted continuously from a wide variety of sources via the mass media. Such stereotypes are used as evaluative standards by individuals in modern society, and 'the point at which accuracy of self-perception becomes apparent . . . may also be the beginning of dissatisfaction with one's body . . . to the extent that one's body differs from the mesomorph image' (Staffieri, 1967). Such stereotypes will undoubtedly affect the way in which an individual perceives his physique and himself. These expectations may result in the transmission of stereotypes so that the child will adjust to the expectations of his somatotype in the course of his development.

Upon examination 'self-esteem' is a highly complex aspect of the person. It has both cognitive components (i.e. awareness) and affective components (i.e. esteem). Traditionally, the concept has been dealt with at two levels of complexity: the concept of one's self in general (i.e. self-concept), and the concept of one's body (i.e. body-image). 'When we speak of high self-esteem, then we shall simply mean that the individual respects himself, considers himself worthy; he does not necessarily consider himself better than others, but he definitely does not consider himself worse; he does not feel that he is the ultimate in perfection, but on the contrary, recognizes his limitations and expects to grow and improve . . .

Low self-esteem, on the other hand, implies self-rejection, self-dissatisfaction, self-contempt. The self-picture is disagreeable, and he wishes it were otherwise' (Rosenberg, 1965). Rosenberg found that participation in extracurricular activities and school clubs was the prerogative of adolescents with high self-esteem. Further, study by Reynolds (1965) on self-esteem, as measured by the Davidson (1960) Adjective Check List, showed certain associations with physique, body size, strength, motor ability and intellectual characteristics of adolescent boys. Sports participants appear to possess a more positive self-concept than non-participants (e.g. Coleman, 1961; Miller, 1967; Buhrmann, 1968).

Another approach to understanding the self has been to examine 'body image'. Kenyon (1968a) in a comparative study of attitudes to physical activities suggested that 'to some extent attitudes towards physical activity are a function of other acquired behavioural dispositions, including body-esteem, self-esteem [and] need for approval'.

The child's conception of his body develops and becomes differentiated as he grows through an interplay of the forces that shape his personality. Witkin (1965) has suggested that development of a differentiated body concept is a manifestation of the child's general progress towards greater psychological complexity. At an early age, the child experiences himself and his body as a 'continuous body field matrix'. As he grows and develops the differences between his body and non-self emerge. During this process, body attitudes are formed. Boys with a high body anxiety were found by Kagan & Moss (1962) to avoid athletic activities and to give an increasing amount of time to intellectual tasks, while Read (1969) demonstrated that constant winners in competitive physical education activities had significantly higher body image and self-concept than constant losers. The task for the physical education teacher may be one of controlling competitive situations in such a way that while benefiting the physically skilled they are not a source of threat to other pupils.

Results from the work of Armstrong and Armstrong (1968) suggest that a relationship exists between physical fitness and body image for adolescent girls but not for boys. The Armstrongs wrote, 'a simple physical fitness score does not discriminate between those boys with a genuine body-image barrier orientation and those without it'. This, they argued, was because boys are socially pressurised to take an active part in physical activity and many will consequently develop a high level of fitness while being quite disinterested. Girls used in their sample were freer to pursue such activity according to their genuine interests. Sex differences in body concept were examined by Smith & Clifton (1962). It was found that women generally held a lower opinion of themselves carrying out certain physical activities than did the men, particularly at running, throwing and jumping. Nevertheless participation in sport apparently has psychologically satisfying and rewarding elements in terms of self and body attitudes for men and women (Schendel 1966; Rehberg, 1969). Snyder and Kivlin (1974) also reported that when comparing women basketball players with gymnasts—and thus implicitly comparing athletes of differing stature and physique—the measures of body image showed that basketball players were as positive as gymnasts; and their cross cultural findings maintained the general finding that athletic participation in all samples was associated with positive self-identity and body-image.

As Witkin et al. (1962) stated, individuals with a more

sophisticated body concept show 'A high level of interest in and respect for the body'.

Perceptual modes have been described by Witkin (1962) as field dependence (i.e. the individual's perception is dominated by the overall organisation of the visual field as discrete) or field independence (i.e. parts of the field are experienced as separate from the organised background and not fused with it). Kane (1972) has suggested that it is conceivable that a field-independent individual may have less difficulty in acquiring skills that depend on body orientation, especially in those skills (i.e. diving and gymnastics) where body awareness is crucial. It is also possible that field dependency may be more of an advantage in the performance of 'open' skills (e.g. team sports) which require the performer to relate the skill or technique to the environment. Rudin (1968) has suggested that the ability to separate the perceptual field into parts is not the same as the ability to perceive an object as distinct from its context. Rudin thus posed the question: 'Is field independence a preferred mode of response which can be changed if the person is motivated to do so, or is it more of a habitual way of responding that the person will inevitably use whether or not he wishes or is motivated to do so? Is field independence a preferential style or is it an ability?'.

Relating this to Witkin's concept of differentiation, Rudin wondered whether a person can switch backwards and forwards from an articulated to a global perceptual style. This suggests a hierarchical system where field independence can be the predominant perceptual mode but certain individuals might be able to switch to field dependence if they so wished. Thus it might be tentatively suggested that individuals involved in sports are more likely than non-participants to demonstrate a predominant mode (i.e. field independence).

Attitude, fitness and skills

With regard to attitude, Kenyon (1968a, 1968b) in his construction of a model characterising physical activities 'as a psychosocial phenomenon', outlined seven domains of attitude towards physical activity. Kenyon's (1968c) own cross cultural study of secondary school pupils in America, Canada, Australia and England showed highly significant differences among the attitude sub-scales. Samples from all countries expressed the most positive attitude towards physical activity as a social experience, as health and fitness, as an aesthetic experience, and as catharsis (i.e. release of tension). Girls expressed a more positive attitude than boys towards physical activity when it was perceived as a social experience, as health and fitness, as an aesthetic experience and as catharsis. Males, on the other hand, expressed more positive attitudes than females towards physical activity perceived as the pursuit of vertigo, and as an ascetic experience. In Britain, Nichols (1971) has reported that favourable attitudes to school games were highly related to games attainment. Using a Lickert version of Kenyon's scales with a sample of fourteen year old children in Ireland, Nichols (1974) noted that no relationship was to be found between specific sports (drawn from games interest factors) and attitude. Similarly school grades did not relate to the attitudinal domains. Girls, however, responded more positively to the aesthetic dimension, while boys responded more positively to the ascetic and vertigo domains. Health and fitness, vertigo and aesthetic dimensions were found to be important components of attitude to physical activity.

There are certain commonalities here with Hendry's (1974) reported findings on post-school samples of university and college education students and 'early leavers'. Results showed that individuals who were involved actively in physical recreation had, not surprisingly, more favourable attitudes towards physical activity. Further, social experience, health and fitness, and catharsis were most favourably and consistently perceived, together with aesthetic experience (especially for women) and asceticism for men.

Fitness may also play its part in whether the individual participates in sports or does not. There is no unequivocal definition covering all aspects of physical fitness. Darling's (1947) definition is, however, sufficiently general to have gained some recognition among research workers. 'Fitness is . . . the ability of the organism to maintain various internal equilibria as closely as possible to the resting state during strenuous exertion and to restore promptly after exercise any equilibriums which have been disturbed'. Therefore, is fitness (however it is defined, measured and assessed) a factor in adolescent sports involvement? Ulbrich (1971) has shown in a study of Prague schoolboys, that cardiovascular fitness is one selecting factor in the sports involvement of adolescent boys. These included sports where general endurance is a limiting factor, sports like skiing, middle distance running, cycling, swimming and canoeing, and sports where cardiovascular fitness is part of the performance but not a limiting factor—football, handball, hockey. Yet as Cumming (1971) wrote, 'If-nothing else, attempts at correlating various fitness performance tests to supposedly precise physiologic measurements make it clear that most tests do not correlate well with the results of another. This is particularly true when athletic performance . . . is correlated with simple measurements of strength, long function and cardio-respiratory performance. *In the average child, the performance of the various athletic functions is so dependent on skill that significant correlations cannot be demonstrated.* The exercise physiologist is virtually unable to predict who is going to do well in a given sporting event from basic laboratory tests . . . Performance tests distinguish the obvious and can tell the athlete from the non-athlete, but are of limited value in the evaluation of physiologic functions in the average population . . . Correlational studies on the average population offer little in the way of defining fitness; they only serve to make one humble, realising how complex the problem of fitness really is' [my italics].

Skill is as open to definition as fitness, but Welford (1968) has defined it thus: 'Skill is concerned with all the factors which go to make up a competent, expert, rapid and accurate performance'. It has been suggested that the development of abilities are prerequisites for successful performance of many different skills. They are not generally task-specific. Fleishman (1964b) in particular makes this distinction between skill and abilities as follows: 'The term 'skill' refers to the level of proficiency on a specific task or a limited group of tasks. As we use the term skill, it is task-oriented. When we talk about proficiency in flying an aeroplane, in operating a turret lathe, or in playing basketball, we are talking about a specific skill'.

In some skills, abilities which contribute to performance early in the learning process are not necessarily the same abilities which contribute to later performance. Thus Fleishman (1967) commented, 'Individuals who are especially good at using certain types of spatial information make rapid progress in the early stages of learning certain kinds of motor tasks, while individuals sensitive to proprioceptive cues do better in tasks requiring precise motor control'. Such ideas are important in so far as it is clear that within the vast range of physical activities available to pupils in schools the possibility of testing basic physical 'abilities' or 'skills' common to them all presented grave difficulties for researchers in measuring pupils' achievement levels other than in a very general way.

Educational factors

McClelland (1961) in comparing preliterate cultures found that those high in need achievement tended to be involved in more competitive and individualistic physical activities. People showing a concern for striving to attain some level of excellence might be involved in movement behaviour as an expression of their forceful personality drives and early learning patterns in the family. But another important factor in adolescents' sports participation is the educational system itself. Within the educational context the most persuasive influence on sports involvement would appear to be academic stream. Nichols (1971) found a high correlation between attainment in games and mental ability. Previous research in this area has shown similar results (e.g. Start, 1966; Hargreaves, 1967), though this relationship may be the consequence of a complex variety of factors.

In addition, as pupils progress through school, interests (or lack of them) harden; a decline in interest in school games across the secondary years has been demonstrated by Ward et al. (1968). Poorer performers show a rapid decline in interest from their first year in secondary school, whilst even good performers indicate a tendency towards diminished interest in team games by the age of fifteen.

A Scottish study

An attempt has recently been made to examine all these factors singly, and in combination, with over 3000 adolescents in 15 comprehensive schools (Hendry, 1975). It was found that more than half the pupils did not voluntarily take part in school sports beyond time-tabled lessons. This leads to an important question in the light of previous evidence discussed above. Are participants and non-participants different 'types' of pupils? A general and consistent trend of differences existed with the intensity of pupils' involvement in school sports, so that there was a relative polarisation of characteristics linked to competitive participation and non-participation. With the mean scores of these two groups situated (relatively) at opposite ends of a theoretical continuum, recreative participants occupied a middle position. In case it should be thought that, even in general terms, competitors, recreatives and non-participants could be described as 'types', it should be noted that the spread of scores obviated to a great extent a typological approach. Neverthelesss, in a way analogous to height or weight differences of men and women (i.e. where a considerable overlap of measures does not blot out the trend of differences between men and women), a pattern of differences among school competitors, recreatives and non-participants was apparent (see below).

From the results of the author's general descriptive findings, therefore, it is possible to confirm and extend existing evidence about adolescents who participate in school sports activities, and to show that competitive, recreative and non-participant pupils are exemplified (albeit with some overlap of scores) by consistent trends

Fig. 1 A general theoretical construct of competitive, recreative and non-participant school pupils' characteristics

in terms of their personal characteristics. The general description of the physically gifted pupil can be given in terms of extraverted qualities, favourable attitudes to sport, muscular physique, physiological capacity and skills ability. The reduced possibility of sports participation by children lacking certain physical and physiological capacities has been described by Durnin (1967) thus: 'The unfit child adopts interests and attitudes leading to a lower level of habitual activity'; while Gordon (1957) summed it up in this manner: 'The athletic field is definitely an important basis of prestige. In order to be a success in the athletic field, you usually have a good physical make-up and a good personality'.

The strong positive self-evaluations which come from identification with the school through sporting events and activities has been described by Coleman (1961). Coleman noted that recognition of athletic prowess gave the individual positive feelings about himself; and adolescent boys who had a high level of physical ability had a much more positive concept of themselves than did those of lesser ability. In the author's reported study active pupils—and especially competitors—were well aware of their own ability and enthusiasm, showed a willingness to attend physical education classes, and had a desire to improve their sports skills; they were also aware of the extra attention given to them by physical education staff.

Body esteem scores showed significant differences between active pupils and non-participants, though again the overlap of scores suggested trends rather than clear-cut differences among groups. Kane (1972), amongst others, has postulated a relationship between self-concept and body image. Arising from Kane's work the question for the physical education teacher may be one of structuring situations so that the pupils derive enjoyment and satisfaction from their experiences. The question of structuring 'appropriate' situations is an important one. At present it would seem as if procedures and situations within the subject produce different effects in and reactions from pupils; reinforcement is positive for some pupils, and negative for others.

Perhaps the current emphasis in the programme is most suited to the outgoing, mesomorphic pupil with a high competitive drive, and strong teacher-identification. This can be linked to suggestions about 'identification' and 'association' of active pupils with school. Competitive school sport in some senses represents ultimate identification with the school and its values of individual achievement and success. Indeed, it might be suggested from Hendry's (1975) study that recreatives reinforce their association with school by being members of the non-sporting clubs (30%) significantly more often than competitors (19%) or non-participants (19.6%). It may be, that lacking the skills or opportunities to represent the school and gain official recognition for this identification, a number of them cement their allegiance by further, more varied, participation in and association with the extracurricular social life of the school.

Roughly one in ten of the competitive pupils had positions of responsibility in the school, whereas the ratio for recreatives and non-participants was approximately one in twenty. Competitive representation appears to enhance prospects of being given social or disciplinary responsibility among fellow pupils, which may reinforce identification with the formal system of values in the school. These social roles made available to competitors may give some initial clue to the processes of reinforcement which lead to the large number of non-participants seeking other success areas within the peer groups in their leisure time.

It would appear then that there are a number of identifiable characteristics in these three broad areas—personal qualities, social background, educational achievements—which distinguish school sports participants from non-participants. It might now be asked if these differences in pupil characteristics combine to create certain assumptions and expectations in teachers which in turn, lead to differentiations in their dealings with pupils according to perceived physical abilities or physique?

Teachers and pupils

Research about teacher-pupil perceptions has previously concentrated almost entirely on the classroom while there is little or no empirical evidence about the interactions between, and perceptions of, physical education teachers and their pupils. Hargreaves (1972), for instance, has suggested that in evaluating pupils in the classroom the teacher gives approval to those pupils who conform to his expectations. Further, Nash (1973) has written: 'The most important point to understand about this evaluation is that it is not wholly (or even mainly) about academic matters . . . Teachers are concerned about their pupils' liveliness, sociability, and simply how likeable they are'. Hargreaves (1972) believes that teachers' perceptual bias is unintentional, but that such differences among pupils as exemplified in speech, appearance, values, attitudes and behaviour in the classroom are used by the teacher as a part of the basis for estimating pupils' intelligence, ability and future potential.

In the same way physical education teachers may use certain perceptual impressions of pupils to construct an overall evaluation of their physical ability and personal qualities, which is conveyed to pupils, setting up matching self estimations in these pupils. There are ample opportunities in the varied educational settings in physical education for processes of teacher-bias to arise: from fleeting impressions, labelling of pupils and the 'halo effect', which are undoubted features of assessments in the classroom. It is possible therefore to pose a number of fundamental questions about this.

   1 How do physical education teachers perceive competitive, recreative and non-participant pupils?
   2 How do pupils view physical education teachers?
   3 How do pupils perceive their own abilities and enthusiasm for physical education?
   4 What 'matching' is there between pupils' self-estimations and the perceptions of physical education teachers?

Since more than half the boys and almost seventy per cent of girls in the author's study were completely non-participant in voluntary extracurricular school sports, it might be asked if there were any clues to be discovered about such widespread non-participation in the relations, expectations and perceptions between physical education teachers and pupils?

On the face of it, there would seem to be less need within physical education for a teaching bias or for pupils to seek the teacher's approval as in the classroom. Not only are physical education teachers free from examination constraints, but they also teach a fairly popular and wide ranging subject—or so it would appear (see Morton-Williams & Finch, 1968).

Taking a different view, however, Hendry (1973, 1975) has suggested that there may be a much greater affinity between the physical education teacher and muscular, physically skilled, competitive children who reveal similarities to the teacher in both physique and behaviour; and by implication, there may be a neglect of children who do not conform to this 'desired' social image.

Teachers of physical education select the pupils who represent the school in sports activities, and it would not be too surprising to find these pupils being rated by teachers as having a very high level of skills ability. Physical ability was not, however, the only important differentiator among competitive pupils, recreative pupils, and non-participants found by Hendry (1975). Enthusiasm, sociability, popularity, competitiveness and reliability were other characteristics which made competitors outstanding. Statistical analyses which were carried out showed that the main elements which distinguished school competitors from other pupils centred around physical education teachers' estimates and pupils' own evaluations of perceived physical abilities and personal qualities.

It has been suggested by Rosenthal & Jacobson (1968) that teachers introduce 'social facilitation' into the learning process by giving differential attention to pupils at both verbal and non-verbal levels. What is being argued here is that the interactions between teacher and pupils, either in the classroom or on the games field, are crucial in conveying 'messages' of praise or disapproval (e.g. Kagan, 1967). These messages subsequently influence different pupils' attitudes, interests and performance in school activities, and this is reflected in a general sense by the favourable perceptions of sports participants held by physical education teachers.

Pupils' views of physical education teachers confirmed a pattern of different perceptions within the school sports context, and, in addition, the self-evaluations of these adolescent pupils revealed the existence of a positive feedback system which led to variations in pupil behaviour, participation in, and attitudes to school sport. Obviously favourable responses from teachers across the school years encourage pupils to continue successfully in sports participation. Yet this same system may depress the self-evaluation of a number of pupils. They do not receive sufficient encouragement from teachers to enhance their self-esteem or physical skills. Over time they cease to participate in school sports, and possibly even in leisure sports away from school. If differential treatment of pupils emerges from consideration of perceived physical abilities what are the implications of physique?

Influences of body type. These considerations about pupils' characteristics and teachers' perceptions are further compounded by an additional analysis by Hendry and Gillies (1978) centring on body type. Adolescents who were more than approximately 1.5 standard deviations from the ponderal index[1] mean were

----

[1] Ponderal index is a measure of body leanness and is calculated thus: $\sqrt[3]{\dfrac{\text{height}}{\text{weight}}}$

categorised as either 'overweight' or 'underweight' and these were compared with an average group (i.e. those who were approximately 0.5 standard deviation within the mean score).

In summary these groups were constituted in the following manner:

	Overweight	Average	Underweight	N
Boys	58	354	36	448
Girls	71	417	50	538

From the extremes of the ponderal index curve 'high' and 'low' ponderal index groups can be identified. A debate could be developed over the basis for extending these terms to indicate 'fatness versus thinness' or 'overweight versus underweight'. This argument is not developed here, however, because the author wishes to draw the reader's attention to the visual aspect of physique (i.e. the comparative 'height versus bulk' appearance). Hence the rather general terms: 'overweight', 'average' and 'underweight' were used in comparing those of 'average' physique with the other two groups of adolescents. Many adolescents appear to worry about their weight (e.g. Sauer, 1966). Not only does obesity represent a potential health hazard, it may also affect the adolescent's social relationships, school performance and emotional adjustment (Hammer, 1965). Stunkard and Mendelson (1967) found that of many behavioural disturbances to which overweight adolescents are subjected, two are unique to obesity: overeating and distortions of body image characterised by a feeling that the body was grotesque, or that it should be regarded with contempt. This can be reinforced by crude witticisms from peers alluding to their obesity. Of course, underweight boys and girls can be as unhappy with themselves as obese adolescents. While they can more readily disguise their physique with careful deployment of clothing they can still feel self-conscious of their slender profiles. Thin adolescent girls are often especially miserable because our culture emphasises the slim but well-proportioned female figure (e.g. Clifford, 1971). For girls outward appearance and their inner self image may be more closely bound together than for males (Douvan & Kane, 1957; Dwyer & Mayer, 1967). 'A girl's self-esteem is anchored to interpersonal relations more often than to achievement, work or skill . . . Achievement is the major worry of boys, and physical appearance and popularity are the centre of girls' concerns', (Douvan & Adleson, 1966).

Boys too have their problems. The ideal masculine body image is to have broad shoulders and chest, a slim waist, well-proportioned arms and legs. But few boys in early adolescence measure up to this ideal. So much emphasis is put on having an athletic build that the boy who is not able to conform feels extremely self-conscious and isolated. Cole (1977) reported a study of adolescent boys all of whom possessed 'inadequate' masculine physiques. The research disclosed that every one of them had some adjustment problems related to self-consciousness about their physical inadequacy. By implication those with an overweight or underweight physique may be less active and less sociable, following more passive pursuits, exhibiting different characteristics and possessing a less clear-cut body concept.

The author's additional analysis (1978) gives some insight into the difficulties experienced by certain pupils within the school setting, and casts further light on to the implications and perceptions associated with particular body-types. It would appear from pupils' comments that processes and situations within school sports produces negative reactions from 'overweight' and 'underweight' pupils. Further, the social context was important in relation to evaluations between persons: the importance of physical attractiveness in teachers' evaluations was reflected in the perceptions of pupils' qualities by physical education teachers. Simply, different body types produced different evaluations from teachers. Underweight adolescents, for instance, were seen by teachers as socially anxious and lacking physical skills (with underweight girls not being seen as particularly competitive) though there was little difference among groups in their actual sports participation. On the other hand, overweight girls were perceived by teachers as being unattractive and this may have subsequent effects on their self (and body) esteem. Further, teachers considered them to lack enthusiasm for sports and show comparatively little competitive drive. Support for such effects can be seen in pupils' self estimates. Pupils' self ratings matched their teachers' perceptions to some extent in that average pupils saw themselves as significantly more physically skilled and having greater enthusiasm for sports than other groups. Yet a desire to improve their physical skills was an aspiration of most pupils irrespective of body type. Thus expectations and perceptions associated with body build, or sports participation are important in understanding the social processes that go on between teacher and pupil.

Whilst it is useful to outline these general trends in teaching interactions, it is at the level of the individual school, and particularly, at the level of the individual pupil that these implications are crucial in social reality. In the next chapter success and failure, expectations and perceptions are examined at an individual level.

Constructed case studies: individual views of school and sport

It does seem as if pupils who are actively involved in sports are differentiated by a number of qualities, attitudes, and interests from those who are non-participants. There are also differences in their self-esteem, and in teachers' perceptions of their qualities and abilities. Yet these variations are essentially general descriptions, and it is only by considering alternative approaches that a way forward can be found in offering a more complete explanation of the effects of these differences on the individual pupil.

Recently educational research has begun to change emphasis from a strictly hypothetico-deductive model, and has moved towards a more sociological-anthropological paradigm in an attempt to understand the social processes involved in teacher-pupil encounters. Illuminative studies of this kind try to uncover the nature of what has happened in social situations (e.g. Glaser & Strauss, 1968).

Within physical education this means using illuminative approaches, and by concentrating on a small number of schools or just one school, studying in detail the whole physical education process. A useful beginning has been made in this direction in the work of Ward and Hardman (1973), and Carroll (1976). This chapter describes one such method of understanding individual pupils' views of school and school sports, by attempting to interpret and construct meanings from the comments of teachers and pupils themselves. In this way the writer takes on the role of a social biographer. The author makes no claim that the evidence here is presented fully from the pupils' perspective, simply that it provides certain insights into individual pupils' standpoints.

The previous chapter revealed that general and consistent trends exist in the characteristics which distinguish between adolescent sports participants and non-participants (although the author's own investigations—Hendry, 1975—suggested that some overlap of scores was apparent in most variables). In case these general findings appear to create an over-simplified picture of the findings, five schools were studied in greater detail (and see appendix for a description of the rationale behind this research approach).

Five schools in focus

Three of the selected schools provided a fairly representative view of suburban, urban, and new town schools in terms of the number of pupils who were competitive, recreative or non-participant in each school. Two other schools were selected because they had 'deviant' characteristics; one urban school had limited opportunities to offer a range of extracurricular sports recreatively; one new town school served a fairly wide geographical area, and reported difficulties in having pupils stay on after school for extracurricular activities (i.e. transport problems). It also had poor facilities. In both cases physical education teachers claimed that the time-table was built round academic teaching and that sports were 'fitted in' thereafter.

The representative schools all had wide extracurricular provision for sports and facilities were good, though there was an element of restriction on pupil participation by teachers' discretion or teachers' estimate of pupils' ability level to gain membership to a sport club or activity.

The 'deviant' schools revealed some difficulties either of provision or facilities for physical activities, and it was clear that in these schools there were problems in maintaining pupil attendance at extracurricular sports activities.

Despite these diverse trends the characteristics of teachers in the various schools were similar, and the qualities and opinions and attitudes of pupils' groups in each school followed a fairly common pattern.

Taking teachers first, it can be stated that irrespective of school provision, their programme's aims are geared towards skills learning, leisure time interests, self and social awareness, and organic development. Enjoyment satisfaction, social understanding and general physical development are the expected pupil effects. Further, they consider that ideally physical education teachers should be knowledgeable of children and their subject, able to communicate their ideas and to win respect.

If physical education teachers share general commonalities of attitude, ideology and teaching approach (perhaps as an outcome of their teacher training experiences: Hendry, 1975) these attitudes of dedication, ability, enthusiasm, and selection may be transferred to their pupils. Certainly the previous chapter highlighted the important association between teachers' perceptions and sports participation.

Pupils also showed a similarity of personal qualities, background and opinion irrespective of school. Within the three groupings (competitive, recreative, non-participant), pupils were remarkably alike in their general pattern of responses in each school. In physical skills and qualities, in their psychological make-up, and in teachers' perceptions general findings were confirmed. It was only in response to questions concerning physical education teachers, and about encouragement and having better facilities that pupils in the two 'deviant' schools and particularly non-participants, indicated more intense opinions: they were concerned about better facilities, more encouragement from teachers, and were more critical of physical education teachers than pupils in the three representative schools.

Constructed case studies

While there was little firm evidence of significant differences among schools, common sense tells us that individual schools *do* possess a distinctive ethos and social context. Thus if such differences can be detected by an observer (or by more 'objective' evidence) yet subjectively pupils do not perceive great differences in the total physical education process, and if their responses to teachers are roughly comparable among schools then clearly this state of affairs warrants closer research.

It may be most useful however to concentrate on two extreme groups: competitive and non-participant adolescents (although a small number of recreatives are included). It was reasoned that whatever forces were operating on these pupils would show up more powerfully or more frequently than in the recreative group. The results from the statistical study showed that the average scores and ratings for recreatives do indeed fall between those of the other two groups in almost every case.

The selection and construction of case studies centred on four types of pupils:

1 those who competed in and out of school;

2 those who did not participate in sport either in or out of school;

3 those who participated in school sport, but did not participate out of school;

4 those who did not participate in school sports but who participated out of school.

Fifty-five adolescents were scrutinised and picked out by the author to demonstrate aspects of the various classifications. The case studies finally written totalled twelve, of which eight are presented in the text. To provide a theoretical framework a number of questions were posed, and by concentrating on two of the five schools used for more detailed examination it was possible to gain some further understanding of the influence of teachers, school and community on the adolescent.

An attempt was made to seek answers to such questions as:

Why does this pupil compete for school but does not even participate recreatively in sports out of school?

What advantages does the pupil see in staying on at school after the compulsory leaving age?

What are the pupils' attitudes to physical education, extra-curricular school sport, leisure pursuits?

How are the most popular boys and girls in class perceived (in four or five words).

What sort of spare time activities are followed beyond homework or housework.

General self-image, and so on.

Thus an extensive and coherent picture of the adolescent in the context of his school and community was developed. These descriptions, constructed in the manner of a biographer, are here called case studies although the term is being used in a rather unusual sense. It should be pointed out that, as far as possible, the words used in the case studies were those used by the pupil himself. Additionally case studies were used to look at teachers' perceptions of pupils and pupils' reactions to the physical education programme in an attempt to tease out the interactions between teacher, pupil, and physical activities at an individual level: an attempt to interpret and construct meanings (cf. Douglas, 1967). These case studies are used to illustrate in more personal terms some of the points argued in earlier chapters of this book.

Case 1 Janet: Non-participant; Recreative; Urban

According to her physical education teacher, Janet is a girl of great athletic ability who likes games. Yet she does not take part in any school sports at all. The teacher describes her as extremely physically able, strong, muscular and reliable, and as more enthusiastic and competitive than average; she is attractive in appearance and comes from a 'good home'. All in all a very complimentary picture, but is it accurate?

Janet describes herself as very enthusiastic; her brother is also very keen, and both parents encourage her. Although she watches little television, she does watch sport, especially athletics, show jumping, swimming and football; and she enjoys physical education classes, the

Categories of the twelve case studies

Number	Pseudonym	Sports participation in school	Physical recreation out of school
*1	Janet	Non-participant	Recreative
*2	Marianne	Competitive	Competitive
3	Angela	Non-participant	Competitive
4	Geraldine	Recreative	Non-participant
*5 and 6	Anna and	Non-participant	Non-participant
	Marie	Competitive	Non-participant
*7	Tommy	Non-participant	Non-participant
*8	Stephen	Competitive	Non-participant
9	Charlie	Non-participant	Recreative
*10	George	Non-participant	Competitive
11	Alan	Recreative	Recreative
*12	Jimmy	Competitive	Non-participant

*denotes case studies described in text.

most important thing about them being the satisfaction she gains from being good at games. Of the sports that school provides she likes dance, gymnastics, swimming, indoor and outdoor team games, tennis and badminton. Able and enthusiastic are certainly accurate descriptions of Janet: but Janet is not competitive. Her scores on the attitude to physical activity inventory are remarkable: on four dimensions—social, health, aestheticism and catharsis—they are well above average, well above even the average for competitive girls, but on the other two, and especially vertigo, they are low. Sport to her is a social activity, graceful to watch, and useful as a relaxation and relief from the rest of life and a way of keeping fit. Excitement, risks, strenuous activity and competition do not appeal to her. She is adamant that she plays all sorts of games at the youth club for 'just fun and enjoyment'. She goes because 'I enjoy going to be with my friends', and her reasons for enjoying physical education are again being with her friends and keeping fit and healthy. It is sociability and fitness, not competition and excitement that she seeks from sport.

Other children (Stephen, Case 8, for instance) represent the school despite not being particularly competitive by nature. Why does Janet not even participate for 'fun and enjoyment'? She does not like school. School is boring, monotonous, useless; the teachers treat them like kids, she's fed up with being told what to do and finds the teachers disinterested in individual children: the sooner she can leave and start working the better. Not surprisingly, she is not expected to get any O-levels (guidance teacher's rating). The enthusiasm her physical education teacher noticed is strictly limited—it is enthusiasm for sports, but not for school or teachers or even physical education teachers. She is scathing in her criticism of the latter—they are, like all the others, not interested in pupils except the very able ones, not sympathetic or approachable and short-tempered into the bargain. Personally she gets less attention than other pupils from teachers. She doesn't like school sports primarily because of the teacher: 'It does not get taught right. The teacher takes you to play rounders, then just goes away because she has no time for the pupils'.

Janet seems to see school solely as a place to learn things (despite her low academic ability and negative school attitude, she sees staying on at school as an advantage because you can 'do O-levels') and she seems to resent not being taught games. She is quite happy playing games just for fun at the youth club, but seems to expect more from school—it seems unlikely that her physical education teacher, who has such a high opinion of her, is at all aware of her resentment. Without an improvement (in accordance with her ideas) in the teaching of physical education, it seems that no amount of enthusiasm for games and sports will make Janet take part in school clubs.

The next case study is of another enthusiastic girl, but this time the pattern of activity is very different.

Case 2 Marianne: Competitive; Competitive; Urban

Marianne competes both in the school and outside it. Is she then a girl whose behaviour is determined primarily by high athletic ability? Her teacher describes her as extremely strong and above average in ability and enthusiasm for physical education and games, and her 600 yard time of 139 seconds confirms this; although not outstanding, she is good. She describes herself, perhaps a little modestly, as of average ability but as very enthusiastic. This she certainly is and her enthusiasm is catholic—on television she watches swimming, football and athletics, in school she plays netball and hockey; out of school she competes in athletics and dancing and after leaving school she hopes to continue dancing and to play ladies' football! In all this she is supported by the undivided attention (she is an only child) and strong encouragement of both parents. The importance of her dancing to her is evident in the attitude to physical activity inventory, where her score on the aesthetic dimension is the highest in the school. She is very interested in graceful sports like skating and dancing and feels very strongly that school should place more importance on them. On the other hand, she states that she very strongly prefers quiet activities like swimming to noisy ones and her score on the vertigo dimension is correspondingly low. When asked why she takes part in all her various activities, it is always the competitive element and having 'complete control of my body' that she stresses.

Marianne identifies strongly with the school—she looks forward to going, finds lots of interesting things going on and does not complain of being treated like a kid. She wants to stay on to try for O-levels; she is in no hurry to start work and feels that the money is less important than having a job you like. Not surprisingly, her attitude to physical education teachers is also very favourable; they are friendly, approachable, fair and interested in all their pupils.

This enthusiasm for school, perhaps deriving from her enthusiasm for sport, leads Marianne to describe herself as a good pupil; cheerful, dependable, friendly, hardworking, clever and eager to learn, and with all this it is not surprising to find that her physical education teacher believes her to come from a 'good home'. What is perhaps surprising is the report of her guidance teacher: Marianne is not very bright, being expected to get no more than one or two O-levels. In addition she comes from an unskilled working class home. It seems that her enthusiasm for sport, and hence for school, and the favourable response she meets from her teachers have given her a slightly inflated estimation of her academic ability.

The last two girls in this section make an interesting comparison, and are dealt with in a combined case study.

Cases 5 and 6 Anna: Non-participant; Non-participant; New Town
Marie: Competitive; Non-participant; New Town

Two girls ran 600 yards several seconds faster than any other girl tested in the school. One of them represents the school in athletics; the other does not participate in any sport in or out of school. What are the differences between Anna and Marie that account for the former's greater involvement in physical activity?

In fact, the two girls are surprisingly alike. This study will first describe their similarities, then look more closely at Anna, and finally compare Marie with this picture.

They are both small girls—Anna is only 4'9" tall, while Marie, at 5'1", is still below average height. They are both just over 6 stone, about 2 stone below the average weight. Not surprisingly, the physical education teacher describes Marie as one of the thinnest girls in the school, whereas Anna's shorter stature compensates for her lightness and she is rated about normal, neither fat nor thin.

Both girls view physical activity largely as a way to keep healthy and are not much attracted by the social aspects of sport. When asked to select the most important things about physical education, they both included 'health and fitness' and 'timing and co-ordination' in their four responses. Neither girl scores highly on the attitude to school questionnaire and their attitudes to physical education teachers are similar—Anna is heavily critical while Marie is a little more favourable than average. Neither takes part in any of the school's non-sporting activities—Anna seems unaware that the school runs a youth club, although many of her classmates attend it—and neither girl intends to continue with any sporting activities after she leaves school.

The analysis so far shows the girls to be alike in many ways, but does indicate a difference in degree; while Marie is rather neutral in her identification with the school and its activities, Anna is strongly antagonistic. She is not expected to get any O-levels and sees staying on at school as 'a waste of time'. She would rather start work as soon as possible, get into the adult world and earn some money. She is not in the least interested in sport and would not go to physical education classes if she had the choice. Her brother and her three sisters are not very keen either, but she says her father encourages her strongly to take part in physical activities. She watches a good deal of television, but it is old

films, westerns, comedies and variety shows that she watches, never sport.
When not watching television, she goes to the cinema, listens to pop music
or goes dancing with a friend. Of all the school activities listed in the
questionnaire the only one she admits to liking is dancing. Her boyfriend,
pop music and 'having a good time' are very important in her life. Personal appearance is important. Anna is described as an attractive and
popular girl. She wishes she were more beautiful, believes that physical
education will improve her 'cleanliness, dress and posture' and describes
the most popular girls as 'brainy and pretty'. Perhaps she thinks that if she
were more pretty she might have more good times and be less bored than
she is.

Anna is academically poor, but even without sports involvement of
any kind after school hours she can run 600 yards as fast as anyone.
If the alternative route to status, through sport rather than study, does
operate, there is surely no-one for whom it would be more appropriate
than Anna.

Marie is not really a sporting type either: her attitude to physical activity, as already said, is particularly oriented to health and fitness but she
also enjoys the ascetic aspects of strenuous exercise and the excitement and
thrills of sport more than most girls. On the other hand, her score is ex-
traordinarily low on the social and cathartic dimensions of the inventory.
Her actual choice of sports bears out these scores. Athletics is her
favourite, the only sport she watches on television, and she also enjoys
gymnastics and swimming: but nothing else—no team games, no tennis,
no skating, or horse-riding. She chooses the individual 'fitness' activities,
the ones whose principal component is fitness and sheer effort, and at the
same time the 'solitary' ones. Not only are they not team games, but even
in competition a runner or a swimmer or a gymnast hardly needs to interact with the other competitors; they are rivals rather than opponents.

Marie describes herself as of average sporting ability but very enthusiastic, and says her two brothers and five sisters are quite keen too.
She would be better at sport if given any encouragement. It is interesting
that Anna, who is not at all enthusiastic, describes her father as very
encouraging, while Marie, who is very keen, says her parents give her no
encouragement. It seems that these girls are perhaps assessing parental
encouragement relative to how much they want rather than how much they
get: Anna is over-encouraged and Marie under-encouraged. Marie spends
her leisure time with a group of girls, plays games and watches a great deal
of sport. She does not spend much time watching television or at the
cinema; pop music, discotheques and boyfriends are not important in her
spare time, but she is seldom bored. Where Anna described the most
popular girls as 'brainy and pretty', Marie puts 'brainy, strong, kind and
pretty'; she relegates 'pretty' to fourth place, and is herself one of the few
girls described as unattractive by the teacher.

Her attitude to school score is higher than Anna's, but is still no more
than average. She is expected to get a few O-grades, but not many, and she
wants to stay on to take them. She wants a job she will like and starting it
soon is not important. School is useful and most subjects are interesting

too, but the teachers treat her like a kid, and she is not sure whether she would rather be in school or out working.

Here then we have the two fastest girls in the school. One is not interested in school, not interested in sport and does not participate in physical activities, preferring coffee-bars and discotheques. The other is fairly happy in school, very keen on physical exercise and runs for the school, though she participates only in school and will stop when she leaves. It is unlikely that Anna would run for a school team even if she fully identified with the values of the school, such is her dislike of physical activities. It is difficult to doubt that Marie's relatively favourable views on school and physical education teachers are partly the result of the school providing the facilities and the encouragement to indulge her interests that she feels she lacks at home.

The other case studies are of boys. The first of these deals with a boy who, in many ways, is like Anna.

Case 7 Tommy: Non-participant; Non-participant; New Town

Tommy does not take part in any games in or out of school, yet he can run very fast—only four of the boys in his school are faster over 600 yards. Why then does he not at least participate in sports?

It might be expected that Tommy dislikes sports, but in fact, he says that he does like them, mentioning athletics, gymnastics and football in particular. To understand his behaviour it is necessary to look more closely at his attitudes to physical education and games in school, and to school itself.

He does not like school. He is fedup with it and welcomes any excuse to stay away (he is, in fact, frequently absent). English is the only academic subject that he ever finds interesting (and that is only sometimes) but his school ability is high, as can be judged from the fact that despite his very low motivation he is nonetheless considered to be a potential A-level candidate. The only other subject he likes is woodwork. He longs to start working and earn money and is not in the least concerned about getting a job that he will like. His opinion of physical education teachers is not very flattering—they are not friendly, and are only interested in the sports teams, having no time for boys like himself who have little interest in games, and thus accord him little attention. His physical education teacher has assessed him as average on every single personality trait, although his ability is clearly high and his enthusiasm clearly low, which suggests that the teacher may have no clear picture of this boy who stays away from school whenever possible and would not go to physical education if he could avoid it.

In his spare time, Tommy watches a lot of television. He enjoys watching sport, especially football, but receives no encouragement to play. He is often bored, spending much of his time with a group of boys who, like himself, play no games. But he seems to be rather a lonely boy—he particularly dislikes the social aspects of games, he does not like dancing and does not think that girl friends matter much, and does not think it is important to have friends to go around with. Family and earning money are the only really important things in life.

Thus it is not a dislike of physical activity, but a distaste for the organisation of school or club that keeps Tommy away from sport—he is able and interested but unrecognised and unencouraged. His physical education teacher apparently has not realised that he is one of the most athletically able boys in the school; his parents give him no encouragement. His own opinions of himself and of his abilities seem depressed by these poor opinions that others hold of him—he believes he is no better than average athletically, he does not realise how fast he can run, he feels restricted and awkward in his movements. Manifestly school has failed in this case; Tommy is not developing his potential, academically or physically.

Case 8 Stephen: Competitive; Non-participant; New Town

Stephen swims competitively for the school, but is not involved in any activities unconnected with the school. He enjoys school, likes and respects his teachers and wants to go to university and get a 'good job'. Here clearly is one subject who contributes greatly to a positive correlation between loyalty to the school and involvement in its sporting activities. What does a closer look reveal about his reasons for competing and not participating?

He is of average height, well-built and, as he puts it himself, 'no weakling'. His physical education teacher considers him average in athletic ability, but not especially enthusiastic. And Stephen agrees with this assessment, more or less, describing himself as fairly vigorous and very fast (in fact, his running speed and agility are very slightly above the average for all boys). He would like to be more vigorous and better at games, but not if this means hard training and athletics. 'I don't enjoy the really strenuous PE classes.' All the same, he would not give up physical education if it was optional, recognising the need of some exercise to keep fit. But this exercise he gets adequately from swimming, and recreatively from hill-walking and occasional games of badminton, and the simple reason why he does not participate outside the school is 'I find adequate exercise at school with swimming, climbing, and I do cycle'.

His identification with the school is really in more intellectual ways—his academic ability is high and he is a member of the debating society and the geology club and plays a horn in the school orchestra. He sees himself as clever, hard-working, dependable, friendly and popular, and believes in the 'sensible' things in life—family, appearance and a good job rather than dancing, pop music, or starting work as soon as possible. To be popular, a boy should be amusing, helpful, intelligent and sensible, just as he sees himself, in fact.

In short, Stephen is a 'good pupil', embodying the academic and social values of school. His physical activities are individual rather than team games, undertaken for fitness and enjoyment, not for ascetic or competitive reasons. But he is a good swimmer and does compete for the school when asked to—a sharp contrast with the 'delinquescent' Derek, also a good swimmer, quoted by Hargreaves (1967) as saying 'I wouldn't swim for this bloody school'.

Case 10 George: Non-participant; Competitive; Urban

An urban working class boy, assessed by teachers as coming from a poor home and having very low academic ability. George plays for a football team in the youth club he goes to. Why does he not play for a school team?

He seems to have physical prowess: according to his physical education teacher he is above average in ability, enthusiasm, reliability, friendliness, competitiveness and in appearance, and is extremely strong. His attitude to sport is remarkable for his very high score on the ascetic dimension—strenuous training and competition—only three boys in the school scored higher. He is also attracted by the social aspects of sport, but not by excitement and risks. His running speed is fairly fast, though not exceptionally so; he describes himself as average in ability, but fairly enthusiastic and would like to be much more vigorous and skilful.

In contrast to his physical ability and enthusiasm, his academic ones are low. He will not be presented for any O-levels, school is utterly boring, and he would rather be working; 'You never get taught anything in the fourth year'. But he is prepared to admit that woodwork and metalwork are useful and interesting while english and maths are useful, and physical education is interesting. School is worthwhile only where it prepares him for work.

It seems that George's negative attitude to school is sufficient to explain his non-participation in school sport. But some other items do not fit this picture so well. Just as his physical education teacher gave a fairly complimentary picture of him, so does he in turn of them. They do not concentrate too much on the good pupils and their teams, but they are friendly, approachable, sympathetic, even-tempered, inspire confidence and he is given reasonable attention by them. Physical education classes are important because of the satisfaction and enjoyment he gets from them, and because they develop team spirit and interests in and out of school—the last two seem a little odd for a boy with such an anti-school attitude. He enjoys physical education classes because 'I enjoy the thrills, speed and excitement of the action'. He enjoys watching football, wrestling, swimming and cricket, and after school he plans to play golf; he also is a member of the school chess club. One last point, when asked which school sporting activities he particularly enjoyed, George only answered yes to swimming: not football, although it seems to be his favourite sport out of school, and although he has an extremely high score for asceticism and hard training.

Case 12 Jimmy: Competitive; Non-participant; Urban

Jimmy is the captain of the school football team; out of school he has no sporting interests. To what extent does he espouse the 'school values' for life in general?

Just over average height and almost a stone below average weight,

Jimmy is particularly strong and a very fast runner, while his general ability and enthusiasm are described as above average. It is his enthusiasm that sets him apart. He has three older brothers, none of whom are very keen on sports (once again, as with Maria and Anna, Cases 5 and 6, this probably means 'compared to me'), but he gets strong encouragement from both his parents. Football is naturally enough his favourite sport, but he also swims for the school, and plays badminton and table-tennis recreatively. He likes pretty nearly every kind of sport; athletics, dance, gymastics, swimming, football, tennis badminton, table-tennis, cycling, wrestling and golf all get a mention somewhere in his answers.

The important things he gets from physical education are that it keeps him fit and gives him enjoyment and more satisfaction than he can get from other school subjects. He likes the classes mainly for the excitement, but it is the chance to do his best and compete that he finds most compelling in sport after school hours. He does not go to any non-sporting school clubs, or to any out-of-school clubs, saying 'don't know anybody in clubs'; his friends all come from school. An extravert, Jimmy is described as friendly, assertive and competitive, very popular, and he claims to get a lot of attention from teachers. He describes himself as popular, fair and honest, a bit of a bully, a good sport but a bad loser—sounds like the ideal competitive team captain!

Along with the enthusiasm for sports goes a positive attitude to school; it is enjoyable, interesting, adult and he would rather be there than out working. All his subjects are interesting, and he is happy to stay on at school 'because you learn a bit more'. It comes as a bit of a surprise to find that he will not be presented for any O-levels at all!

Academically Jimmy is very poor, but his enthusiasm for sport has been harnessed by the school, making him football captain, and producing in him a strongly positive attitude to school. For once, at least, the alternative to status has certainly worked.

Concluding comments. Observational studies examine real-life situations looking for causal relationships and influences, while statistical correlational research need not necessarily mean that causal connections exist. A weakness of observational research, however, is that the original statistical correlations or significant differences are often not established at all. Observers frequently admit that different researchers might well derive different events or aspects of events to record and interpret.

The constructed case studies were extracted, as it were, from a larger statistical study, so that the use to which the case studies can be put is intimately bound up with the overall results of that investigation. It seems possible to suggest that constructed case studies (corroborated by a statistical skeleton) can provide theoretical insights of their own by forcing the researcher (and reader) to concentrate on individuals, and perhaps especially the 'atypical' ones.

In conclusion case studies remind us in very personal terms that school sports can serve a useful function for some adolescents, but also serve—in conjunction with the school system generally—to drive some adolescents to seek out other leisure interests. They also raise questions about both the teaching of physical education and teacher-pupil relations. This may be considered to be important by some if there is an intimate association between school sport and physical recreation: and if, when the 'pupil' role is discarded it is substituted by a 'pop' or 'street corner' role in adolescence.

CHAPTER 6

Extracurricular activities and leisure: a clash of values

Extracurricular activities are those activities or studies which do not form a part of the formal school curriculum. A tremendous variety and range of activities can be found in this category; these may include clubs and societies for photography, stamp collecting, chess, model making, gardening, angling, athletics, sport and games of all kinds. The Newsom Report (1963) stated that 'These activities, outside the limits of lesson times, are a valuable and distinctive feature of school life', and that in present day society, 'Most schools would agree in attaching importance to experiences offered outside the formal lesson programme'.

In most schools extracurricular activities are teacher-initiated and organised. Thus the extent to which staff feel inclined (and are able) to provide a variety of activities, largely determine the pupils' opportunity for extracurricular participation. Monks (1968) found, however, that sixty percent of all teachers (in a sample of 331 schools) did take part in extracurricular activities.

Reid (1972) stated that men teachers as a group were more involved in these activities than women. Most time was spent pursuing extracurricular activities by single men, least time was spent by married women. The low level of involvement of women generally may have something to do with the low participation of girls in extracurricular activities.

In a report by the National Foundation for Educational Research (1972) twelve comprehensive schools were studied in considerable detail. From this Ross (1973) described the physical education facilities and their use in out-of-school hours, and which fifteen-sixteen year old pupils had played in sports teams in each of the twelve schools. The findings showed that the pupils in small comprehensive schools were taught the major physical sports and skills and had access to all the usual facilities, equally with those in large schools. However the small schools were more restricted in the range of minor activities (e.g. rounders, volleyball) offered. Greater use was made after hours of the facilities for sport and physical education in urban than in rural schools, both by the pupils themselves and by other organisations. In large schools pupils had rather less opportunity for gaining a place in a school team but this was balanced to some extent by the fact that the opportunity of playing for house or form was the same in the large as in the small schools. The able and middle class pupils were more often team members in all schools but participation was more evenly spread over the pupils in the mixed ability schools than in the others.

Evidence from a study by Barker and Gump (1964) into the effect of school size on participation in extracurricular activities, provided positive proof that although smaller schools may not permit a wider range of activities than the larger school, level and extent of participation was greater.

From the results of Saunders and Witherington's (1970) study there was little evidence to suggest that the larger schools offer either a wider range of activities or a greater number of opportunities to participate. So far as pupil participation in extracurricular physical activities was concerned, a greater percentage of pupils in small schools had participated and had continued to participate more frequently than their counterparts in large schools. 'Nearly all the big existing comprehensive schools appear to be too big to fulfil the social aspect of their educational function properly' (Pedley, 1956).

Saunders and Witherington indicated that there was little evidence to suggest that larger schools offer a wider range of activities or a greater number of opportunities to participate. They suggested that this is partly explained by three factors. Firstly, that a larger compliment of staff does not necessarily generate a greater number of supervised extracurricular activities. Secondly, that a small school has had much opportunity to develop a wide range of activities which may not depend on facilities (e.g. cross-country running, Duke of Edinburgh's Award Scheme). Thirdly, that the structure of inter-school competition creates a situation where small schools have equal opportunity of competing in similar activities at all levels and will proportionately offer greater opportunity to a larger number of pupils in the school. The third point is particularly relevant to extracurricular physical activities but does not apply to hobbies or pursuits of a non-competitive nature.

It is notable that the type of school may influence the emphasis given to certain kinds of extracurricular activities. From Emmett's

(1971) work, the trend is for sport-loving youngsters to be more commonly of middle class rather than of working class origin. Since the majority of the children of middle class origin were predominantly found in what may be termed 'selective schools' it is not surprising to find that the type of extracurricular activity most common to the 'selective school' was sport orientated. Embodied in this is the notion that 'games provide for the individual a preparation for life or character building . . . and . . . foster the corporate spirit of loyalty, harmony and purpose' (Copeland, 1972).

Reid (1972) has suggested that the central objective of the comprehensive school is to 'involve' a wide variety of pupils as fully as possible. It is therefore suggested that emphasis is theoretically placed on the mixing of pupils both inside and outside the teaching situation. It is interesting to ask if comprehensive schools have in practice achieved social and academic integration. The principle of social integration may be defined as providing a situation 'where children of varied abilities and diverse social backgrounds attend a common school which affords increasing opportunity for developing co-operative and satisfying social relationships' (Saunders & Witherington, 1970). Thus Reid (1972) has posed a provocative question in evaluating the extent to which extracurricular activities involve social integration when she asked: 'Why don't a higher percentage of the able pupils belong to activities other than the "prestige" activities?' These 'prestige' activities were either sports teams or school choirs, and it was suggested that in some schools at least the integrating function of such activities for pupils may be sacrificed to achieve a higher level of competitive performance for the chosen few. In this connection, Leigh (1971) has pointed out that though schools may provide a wide range of activities relatively few pupils are members of these extracurricular clubs.

Another benefit of pupil involvement is that he is placed in a more relaxed, informal relationship with the teacher in charge than might be possible in the classroom situation. This closer relationship works both ways, and as Shipman (1968) said, 'School clubs and societies allow children to pursue interests outside the classroom, but they also enable staff to get closer to children than is sanctioned in the classroom'. The Newsom Report also supported this idea: 'there is a strengthening effect . . . in teachers getting to know their pupils in a different more intimate companionship'.

However, attracting many youngsters to extracurricular activities is no mean task; the activities are not usually based on what the 'clients' want, rather they are dictated by the specialist skills and interests among the available staff.

There are of course numerous other factors which influence or affect participation in extracurricular activities: after school employment, membership of leisure activities unconnected with school and unsympathetic parental attitudes towards school activities may deter many from participating. The distance of the parental home from school is also important: pupils may have to travel long distances from scattered areas, in which case they may not be able to stay on late after school. The nature of school facilities is another limiting factor; a new school with games hall, gymnasium, swimming pool and generally good facilities for arts, crafts and music can be expected to offer much more than an old school in poor, cramped quarters.

Details concerning extracurricular sports

King (1973) has discussed games and extracurricular activities in some detail. He found that boys were provided with a larger number of games than girls. The number of games played by both boys and girls was highest in the comprehensive schools, lowest in the secondary modern schools.

Games were formalised in schools by means of publicity: notice boards, results published in school magazines, and announcements at morning assemblies. The ritualisation of the games system was extensive: awards were given in the form of badges, ties and sashes for playing in a school team. This ritualism was lowest in girls' schools and in mixed secondary modern schools.

In single sex schools, (with the exception of boys' grammar schools), middle class pupils were more often members of school teams than working class pupils. This class difference was not consistent in mixed schools, but here it was found that boys were almost always more often team members than girls. These sex differences can be partly explained by the different opportunities available for team membership, in that there were generally more team places for boys than girls. King suggested that in mixed schools team membership, and perhaps sport in general, has strong masculine connotations and so consistent class differences did not arise. He also stated that 'There was no simple relationship between the number of teams provided by a school and the percentage of pupils playing for school teams. This is probably partly due to the concentration of such teams for older pupils and also suggests that when more teams exist the same pupils tend to join several of them'. King suggested that the games system generates a large number of minor success roles: team member, team captain and so on, which can be linked to a general identification of the school by the pupils involved.

Extracurricular activities and leisure. Since the academic and social advantage of comprehensive schools are still hotly debated it might be interesting to consider whether the ideology of a classless society is evident in the extracurricular life of comprehensive schools. A problem that has been of some concern to educationalists, headmasters and teachers of physical education in Britain, is why an increasing number of pupils in secondary schools do not participate in extracurricular physical and sports activities. It might seem superficially that non-participation is a symptom of the more general problem of 'school rejection' among many pupils of this age range in secondary schools (Hargreaves, 1967; Reid, 1972).

The evidence from the study of secondary school pupils detailed in Chapter 3 (pp. 46–47) revealed that the emphasis in extracurricular physical and sports activities follows a pattern similar to that of the 'official' time-tabled programme. That is, while the provision of activities was found to be generous and the range of activities wide, yet there were few activities offered in addition to competitive sports and solely for recreational reasons. In other words 'official' activities were predominant and competition and selection were stressed.

It was reported that in the running of extracurricular activities by teachers of physical education the teaching situation was 'teacher dominated' and a great deal of emphasis placed upon a pupil's competitive ability. When teachers were asked about the way they taught physical education they perceived their task as leisure preparation, the development of pupil self-awareness, and developing social relationships, in addition to the development of physical skills and competitive sports abilities. Moreover they reported that their aims were the satisfaction and success of *all* pupils rather than the physical and sporting achievements of the few.

Pupils fell into two clear groups: those who chose to participate and those who did not. The participators were found to be enthusiastic about sports; they stressed competitive ability, physical skills, success in achievement and a desire to improve their skills. The non-participators saw sport in school as conferring a certain prestige on those pupils who were good at it. They reported that physical education teachers concentrated upon a few pupils rather than upon them all. While some said they 'had a lot of things to do' or were 'not interested' when asked about physical and sports activities outside school hours, yet many said they enjoyed the sports activities in themselves and would like to improve their skills. Almost all pupils thought that teachers of physical education were 'friendly and approachable', but also they were said to be 'aggressive and competitive'. The participant pupils said teachers gave them confidence but non-participant pupils said the opposite.

Using Kenyon's (1968) attitude inventory, Hendry (1975) found that most pupils emphasised that their attitudes to sports centred around enjoyable social experiences and thrill and excitement. Additionally, girls favoured sports involving an aesthetic experience, while competitors held strong favourable attitudes towards sports concerned with strenuous training and competition (i.e. asceticism). Boys perceived the outcomes of the school's physical education programme as giving them enjoyment, fitness, satisfaction through success, the development of wide ranging interests and relaxation from the more formal school curriculum. Girls while endorsing health and fitness and enjoyment added an important dimension, that of team spirit and 'feelings of belonging' which can come from corporate sports participation.

As an extension of these findings, all types of pupils gave fitness and health as their prime reason for participation in compulsory time-tabled physical education. Yet while in voluntary extracurricular activities, fitness continued to be important to recreative participants, competitors (perhaps not surprisingly) stressed competitive reasons for participation. In leisure sports competitors continued to emphasise the need to satisfy competitive urges, while other adolescents were involved for social reasons (association with friends, meeting people etc.) and for excitement. Leisure sports appear to offer opportunities for adolescents (from their perspective) to socialise with other teenagers, fulfil competitive drives, seek thrills and excitement via legitimate means and to maintain a level of fitness and health.

Non-participants expressed a lack of interest in the procedures of the time-tabled programme whilst claiming to find some inherent appeal in actual physical activities. About half of them stressed that they had too many other things to do as their reason for not participating in schools' extracurricular sports activities, while another twenty per cent mentioned a lack of interest in sports. Leisure non-participants were not interested and not prepared to devote time to physical recreation and sports. They especially stressed that they preferred to be 'doing other things' related to friends, pop music, discotheques rather than being involved in sports.

It is true to say that in secondary education, schools are stratified in terms of an authority structure and in terms of academic and non-academic subjects. In other words knowledge and activities are stratified according to evaluations of what is worthwhile knowledge and activity. This is so in spite of attempts to reorganise secondary education along comprehensive lines and in spite of alternative approaches to curriculum development and the notion of community-schooling (Midwinter, 1972, 1975; Illich, 1971; Thorpe, 1973).

In British secondary schools, teachers and pupils are caught up in a hierarchical social structure. An experience of hierarchy hence permeates everyday school routines and is embodied in the differential distribution of educational achievement according to social class (Little & Westergaard, 1966). The study of one large mixed comprehensive by Keddie (1971) showed that even when attempts are made to break down the hierarchy of subjects and the ranking of knowledge, pupils are still classified by teachers according to the social determinants of academic success.

All hierarchical systems inherently contain competitiveness and aggressiveness because at the top rewards are high and scarce. Schools are no exception. The rewards of ordinary and higher level certificates linked to further and higher education and occupational success are scarce values, in theory open to competition. There are many pupils for whom the competitive system is not an open one in Britain because they are 'losers' before the race begins, mainly because of social determinants of educational achievement like wealth, property and social class. The system of secondary education processes 'winners and losers' and it is necessary to commit participants to competing and accepting the results. Not only pupils but also teachers must have some degree of commitment to the system and this is achieved by getting participants to believe in the 'rightness' of it. In other words, participants hold common values, and hence maintain a system which brings rewards for 'successful' teachers and pupils.

Moreover, the system is not without its sanctions. There is a coercive side to all organisation even though in secondary schools today coercion is limited, especially physical coercion. Sanctions such as educational and occupational failure in monetary terms are not.

In order for the values of competitiveness, monetary rewards and success to be maintained there are public ceremonies in which the common values can be collectively re-affirmed. In all social organisations re-affirmation of core values takes place in public rituals (Goffman, 1959). In secondary schools, the collective rituals of morning assembly, prize-giving ceremony, and sports day traditionally have been common. Also everyday organisational routines like age-sets, sex-sets and for the recalcitrants the visit to the headmaster for punishment, are collective rituals. The separation of academic pupils from non-academic; the 'bright' from the 'not so bright' are also rituals.

The concept of ritual means an event or happening; arrangement or occasion, which has meaning for the individual and the collectivity beyond the merely physical or specific situational sense. A ritual communicates significance beyond the mere obviousness of the situation. A sports-day gathering of staff, pupils, parents and local community dignitaries means more than watching competitors engage in physical sports. It is also about 'belonging to the school', 'competing for the house' or for the school, 'the pride of your parents', and so on.

The main point about school rituals is that they all embody a fundamental social rule, namely the rule of separation (Douglas, 1966). Consider for instance the morning assembly. In the procedures adopted and the atmosphere created it separates school from non-school. The school environment is 'sacralised' by a prayer and a hymn and a firm separation made at the start of the day between the 'sacred' environment of school and the 'profane' world outside. Rituals like age-setting and sex-setting or ability-setting clearly embody separation of young and old, male from female, bright from non-bright. Selection and streaming is a major aspect of this ritualised separation of winners and losers.

Hierarchy and sport. The study of physical education and sports activities by the author (1975) showed how the everyday routines of teachers of physical education and pupils exemplified such rituals. The stress upon competition and ability; upon physical status and the attainments of the few; the prestige of certain activities and representing the school, all reveal the importance of hierarchy, rituals and sports activities.

Moreover, given the congruency of the social relations of school and wider society, the significance of sports activities in the school is enhanced because sports-success is highly visible and judged worthwhile by members of wider society. Achievements in physical activities and in sport enhances the reputation of the school in the eyes of 'significant others' and the 'generalised other' (i.e. parents, headmasters and the wider community in which the school is located: Hendry, 1975a).

Most importantly in sport there are always 'winners and losers', either at the individual, team, house or school level. Quite visibly, because of competition, striving and success, some receive rewards and deserve them because they have won, but others have lost and hence do not receive rewards nor deserve them. This is a visible lesson that is seen by pupils, parents and others and hence is crucial in supporting those beliefs which maintain the legitimacy of the system.

Ceremonies like the assembly, prize-giving and so on celebrate cherished values like competitive striving, aggression, and success, but physical activities and sports embody them in everyday routines. Sport fits into school rituals because it fundamentally separates pupils into winners and losers, inferior and superior. It teaches lessons which apply to life in general given a particular form of social organisation of society in Britain. At the school assembly the successful pupil or team is 'separated' from the rest by name and an identity as a 'winner' is established.

Teachers of physical education are significant within the hierarchical structure of the school because of their ambiguous position. Typically teachers of physical education are accorded low status and feel themselves to be of low esteem in the eyes of significant others. Typically, they 'separate' themselves by dress, language, manner and speech and often by physical location in the school (Hendry, 1975a). Because of this status ambiguity and a sense of deviant identity they may seek to enhance their status and sense of self-esteem by sports success. Also it is necessary for them to reveal to others their own merit in order to secure career enhancement. Because sport can lend itself so easily to competitive ability, and striving for success, teachers of physical education quite simply fit into the hierarchical structure of the school and they celebrate its attendant rituals. Physical education and sports success brings honour to the school and this is visible in the eyes of all those who count; the significant others of the school, the significant others outside of school and the generalised other, i.e. wider, society.

Thus, while teachers of physical education may have innovatory intentions, acquired in modern teacher training institutions and embodied in contemporary philosophies of education, yet they are caught up in a hierarchical structure of school social relations; teaching styles, curriculum routines and attendant rituals.

Those pupils who participate in extracurricular physical and sports activities are also implicated in the hierarchical system in various ways. These pupils guide their conduct in academic and in sports activities according to the rules of appropriateness for the situation in which they are involved. Because of their adherence to rules of appropriateness rewards flow to them. It can be argued that, for pupils who are the comprehensive school's equivalent of Hargreaves' (1967) pro-school subculture, sports might be seen not only as an opportunity for recreation but also as an occasion for

demonstrating a wide range of social skills and further identification with the school's values (Spady, 1970). So sport becomes
another manifestation of school culture. They receive more attention from teachers and in the eyes of other pupils they are both
visibly and verbally rewarded. Often they are the 'accolytes of the
ceremonies' as prefects and team and house captains and of course
they are frequently involved in ceremonies as recipients of prizes
and commendations. Moreover they have some power, albeit
limited, in the hierarchical structure of the school and they enjoy
status in the eyes of other pupils and members of staff (Hendry,
1975).

Pupil choice. Pupils who do not participate in extracurricular
activities are aware that participant pupils are implicated in the
school hierarchical structure and that they receive differential
rewards. Moreover, they are aware that rewards accrue to participants because of their success in competitive striving and that
their success brings honour to the school and teachers of physical
education.

The strength and pervasiveness of the dominant authority
structure and culture (that is, of the school system) is exemplified
by the conduct of physical education teachers. They state a philosophy of physical education quite contrary to the traditional
philosophy of hard physical exercise, and moreover 'devalue'
competitive ability, physical skills, the attainment of the few etc.
However, in everyday routines they support and celebrate the
dominant authority structure which is imposed and maintained.
From their viewpoint this is legitimate and rewarding because of
the relationship between the authority structure of the school, the
way sport 'fits' the ritualisation of values, and the way success
enhances the honour of the school and helps their own careers.

From the viewpoint of pupils who participate it is also rewarding
and legitimate. There is some evidence that pupils who 'do well' in
school and stay on and take academic subjects, are by and large the
pupils who take part in extracurricular subjects, including physical
and sports activities (Start, 1966; Reid, 1972; Hendry, 1975).

From the viewpoint of those who do not take part, the system is
neither legitimate nor rewarding. The choice of pupils not to
celebrate school rituals in extracurricular activities embodies a
critique of the dominant authority structure and its values. But it is
a two pronged critique; comprised of experiences within the school
but formed and sustained by social relations and culture outside of
school.

The pupils who choose not to participate in extracurricular

physical and sports activities are either 'too busy doing other things' or they say they are 'not interested'. This is because teaching styles and activities are extensions of school. If this is related to the decline in participation in morning assembly, prize-giving ceremonies and sports days then a pattern begins to emerge. Even if all secondary schools have not abandoned assembly, there is some evidence that while there is no 'actual' withdrawal by pupils, yet there is a studied indifference. The same can be suggested for prize-giving and sports day celebrations. At many schools only competitors participate in sports days because of the large number of pupils who stay away from school when they are supposedly attending sports days.

Pupils who choose not to participate are saying 'We are critical of those rituals which celebrate hierarchical authority and the rule of separation into "winners and losers". We are critical of an authority system based on competitive values and the attainments of a few. We are critical of a system which distributes rewards to the same winners for most of the time both in school and in wider society.'

Thus the choice not to participate in extracurricular activities but to choose to celebrate their own rituals is part of an overall pattern of rejection by secondary pupils of the authority and rewards that the traditional hierarchical system sustains. It is a critique of the system that extends to the hierarchy of knowledge, subjects and status both in school and society.

The rituals that non-participant pupils celebrate are in 'pop culture'. These rituals can be clearly seen in football supporters' behaviour, or at a Saturday night pop concert in the local stadium which proceeds through certain ritualised and fairly predictable stages from start to frenzied finish. There is still the fundamental social rule of separation but it is the rule of separation of young from old or youth from traditional authority.

The problem is complicated because it is a product of the complex relationships outlined above between school and society. Moreover it is complicated because a specific 'mechanism of disjunction' can be identified that is responsible for the problem. For example the disjunction between the ideology of com-prehensive education and the actual experiences of pupils in secondary schools.

The dominant ideology stresses 'equality of opportunity for rewards' and then operates within the framework of a hierarchical system. This is then experienced by many pupils as patently false, or at best a distortion of reality and a contradiction. Also, the ideology of teachers of physical education stresses social relationships, enthusiasm, the heightening of self-awareness and so on, then in practice one finds the celebration of hierarchical rituals. The culmination of this is a blurring of the distinction between school and non-school. In assembly for example the ritual rule is a separation of school from non-school but then pupils experience what should be the epitome of this distinction, i.e. extracurricular activities, as an extension of school. Again there is ambiguity and disjunction. This is compounded by pupils' orientations which underline even more the distinction between school and non-school. Pupils whose family and social class relations maintain traditional orientations towards school can manage the disjunction because of their parents' beliefs that furnish legitimacy, and also by the allurement of rewards both in school and in occupational terms exemplified by their own parents' achievements and their aspirations for their children. When these are lacking and orientations of pupils are formed and maintained by a peer group linked to youth culture, then criticism of the prevailing authority structure and its rituals is paramount. This it can be suggested helps us to understand the situation of physical education and sports activities in secondary education. What is occurring is not school rejection/acceptance or participation/non-participation, but a critique of a traditional authority structure and attendant rituals epitomised in school physical education and sports activities.

In order to sustain this argument one has only to examine changes that have occurred in secondary schools. Collective rituals like assemblies, sports days, prize distributions and so on have declined and guidance and counselling have developed. These are no less rituals, in the sense of celebrating cherished values and communicating meanings beyond the situationally specific and physical sense of the occasion. Again the fundamental rule of separation is operating, the separation of the problem boy or girl from the non-problem pupils. The separation of the 'social' side of the teachers' function from the teaching function; the separation of guidance and counselling from 'normal' teaching duties; a special room, special training, special titles and allowances.

Just as the collective rituals were concerned to communicate meanings to the collectivity and to individuals, so the therapeutic rituals of guidance and counselling seek to perform the same function.

The pattern established in school sport seems to repeat itself in leisure sport. Active pupils perceive more encouragement from teachers to engage in community sports, have stronger intentions of pursuing sports in their post-school life, and are less likely to watch television regularly (Hendry, 1975). So, in the sphere of sport there seems to be strong links between school and community. Relatively few active schoolboys were found by the author to be non-participant out of school, and more than half the active schoolgirls had dual sports involvement. The pattern for school non-participants tended to be towards continued non-involvement in sport out of school.

This evidence certainly supports the idea of pro- and anti-school subcultures, where reinforcement comes from physical education staff who mirror the achievement ideology of their classroom colleagues. But this rejection of sports participation seems to generalise more widely to include leisure participation, and not simply school participation.

Many observers have commented on the increasing importance for the developing adolescent of activities which allow continued interaction with peers. Most replies given by non-participants about the nature of their leisure pursuits included activities which were designed to cater almost exclusively for adolescents or which were undertaken in groups: discotheques, dances, youth clubs, drinking, dating, going 'on the town', or 'hanging around' with friends. Participation in physical activities may not be sufficiently rewarding to fit into this pattern of corporate leisure for many teenagers. Boys particularly were more group conscious in their leisure.

Of course active adolescents also involve themselves in non-sporting pursuits which enables them to meet their friends and socialise outside the home, perhaps without threat of competition and rivalry. The interesting point, however, was their dual involvement—sports to satisfy their competitive drive, or for fitness, and to ensure association with the world of adults—non-sporting activities aligning them to their peers, and centring round common interests. So sports participants have 'a foot in both camps'. They have more opportunity to experience a wide range of social roles, and thus perhaps show a greater versatility in their social relations than non-participants. It is not without significance that Hargreaves (1972) wrote: 'In turning to commercial enterprises for leisure activities, or in creating their own . . . adolescents are in a vulnerable position with respect to commercial exploitation and are likely to reduce the amount of informal contact with responsible and caring adults'. These ideas lead back to the provision made by schools for the education of adolescents: 'The influence of thousands of hours in schools given to arts and crafts and to physical education and cultural development was only partially discernible in post-school leisure interests' (Simpson, 1973).

So it can be suggested that attempts within the extracurricular life of comprehensive schools to educate pupils towards 'worthwhile' leisure pursuits can be divisive and reinforce different pupil groupings. The associations among school sports, social class and academic ability reported by Reid (1972) were reflected in both school and leisure sports in Hendry's findings. Of course individual pupils from working class backgrounds and of poorer academic ability *do* represent the school in physical activities. Nevertheless, pupils who identified most closely with school values were most actively involved in extracurricular activities: these pupils are rewarded in a variety of ways for their identification and association with school, and, in turn, they form a distinct subculture within the school: a larger group are alienated from school and turn to pop culture and peers in their leisure time.

Perhaps only in leisure pursuits—and not in the structured and strictured atmosphere of school—do many adolescents seek their self identity, and hence search out activities, sporting or nonsporting, which fulfil their quest for excitement, success and acceptance.

DIMENSION 3
LEISURE

CHAPTER 7

Society and Leisure

> As a society we have been astonishingly successful in ignoring biology. Indeed, it is precisely as the maturity of the young has been accelerated . . . that we have kept them in very longer tutelage and dependence. This is a tribute to the power of social institutions and the organization of the mature. Perhaps, indeed, they have been kept in ever longer subordination just because *they* are more mature and consequently threatening to the old. Whatever biological changes may have occurred over the past century, where society does not permit the adolescent to assume a social role compatible with his physical and intellectual development, but keeps him dependent and irresponsible at home, adult maturity is come by with more difficulty (Musgrove, 1964).

Musgrove further suggested that the contemporary social order and adult social attitudes are based, if not upon hypocrisy, then on gigantic myths concerning the needs and nature of the young. Yet young people in their leisure may reflect versions of adult society at play, and indeed, may mirror subcultural patterns which are similar to adult pursuits though cast within adolescent terms.

The intention in this dimension is to examine the leisure activities of different groups of young people by considering some of the provision for adolescent leisure made by society; then, in the second chapter by studying how young people's leisure interests reflect particular life-styles developed within certain subcultures of society.

Adolescence is a peak time of leisure needs. Young people have more free time and perhaps less responsibility than at any other time of their lives. But those under sixteen years of age and those 'staying on' at school are restricted by lack of spending power, lack of transport, and by police and parental limitations. Sillitoe (1969) has reported on the tremendous reduction in physical recreation after adolescence. Interest seems to decline markedly with marriage for young women, and drops drastically after the birth of the first child for men. Clearly home-making and the family turn young married couples in towards the family unit and away from more corporate leisure interests. Additionally, three quarters of young people interviewed in Sillitoe's enquiry said they were in favour of age segregation in clubs and leisure pursuits. On the basis of such findings it might appear that young people actually desire a separate youth culture, further extending the so-called 'generation gap'. Those subcultures comprising their peers and excluding adults can perhaps be seen as a reaction against their exclusion from certain adult activities.

But such an interpretation would be naive and limited without an exploration of general leisure provision in society, seen in relation to the leisure activities of various groups of adolescents. Work and leisure are both important elements in people's lives. The interplay between demands made by work and demands the individual makes upon his leisure influences the life-rhythm. Leisure is an activity which is absorbing to the participant (and to the theorist) since patterns and underlying structures can be noted which may reflect life-styles and provide clues to a general understanding of society.

Any discussion of leisure is tied up with the question of freedom (i.e. what we do when we can exercise choice). There are many limitations imposed even when one can make a choice. Freedom is circumscribed by physical circumstances, local cultural expectations and individual limitations.

Further, Glasser (1970) suggested that an individual's or group's choice of leisure reflects the stage they have reached in their search for a desirable identity. He shows how the 'parcelling up' of time in leisure means one takes on obligations and as a result one could be considered as having 'no leisure'. (As such, 'true leisure' must mean the time when there are no claims on one's time being made and the available choice of activity presents no attraction.) He assumes, therefore, that this self-imposed deadend is intolerable and thus thinks it is quite understandable that people take on leisure obligations in line with their desired identity and life-style, and which are, at the same time, circumscribed by local cultural norms and physical environment.

Society plans for leisure

It has been suggested that leisure time encompasses four spheres of living (Elias & Dunning, 1967):

1. Private work and family management: this includes domestic planning and provision, and consumes greater time and skill as

standards of living increase.

2. Rest: this means recuperating, doing little or nothing: sitting, sleeping, smoking, knitting or simply pottering around.

3. Sociability: this requires considerable effort, and variations by social class can mean, for example, visiting in-laws, going to pubs, clubs, or restaurants.

4. Play (mimetic sphere): this can encompass football or bridge; going to sporting spectacles, theatre, races or cinema; hunting, fishing, shooting, dancing and so on.

The mimetic sphere may be vitally important in producing opportunities for tension and excitement, through football, pop festivals, and other activities sanctioned to allow catharsis in the young.

Leisure is seen both as of ultimate value and as a social problem. 'The ever decreasing length of the average working day suggests that the problems of leisure will increasingly come to the forefront of both theoretical and practical interest' (Giddens, 1964). It may become apparent that much of the concern directed towards leisure is related to the breakdown of social stability, and leisure may be seen as a stabilizing function in society. Kraus (1967), for example, has advocated 'constructive' recreation programmes as an outlet for aggression evident in rioting, football hooliganism and the like. But it is important to pursue the idea of possible differences in leisure life-styles as a reflection of subcultural values and general patterns of living. A 'leisure democracy' thesis has been proposed by a number of sociologists. Roberts (1970) suggested that 'As far as the distribution of leisure is concerned Britain can be called a democratic society. Whereas the distribution of income and wealth is decidedly unequal, leisure is spread remarkably evenly through the various social strata.'

As a result of leisure *time* being distributed fairly evenly throughout society, Britain has been described as egalitarian in the sense that there exists no sharp cleavages distinguishing the leisure of one class from another. In spite of differences in income and financial resources that exist, leisure pursuits adopted throughout society are portrayed as being similar to a remarkable degree. Emmett (1970) also stated that there is some evidence that working class people emulate middle class recreational activities, yet significantly she neglected to specify the nature of such evidence! Thus leisure provision tends to be structured in a manner that visualises potential users of facilities as exhibiting the characteristics of affluence, mobility and an ability to make rational selections among the leisure alternatives offered to them. There also appears to be an assumption that social integration into the middle classes is the ultimate goal to which the working classes aspire. Social class, then, is seen as largely irrelevant and appears to have been disregarded in planning for leisure.

So called 'evidence' of this progressive classlessness is to be found, over time, throughout its literature. Orwell (1934), for instance, declared that 'in tastes, habits, manners and outlook the working class and the middle class are drawing together.' However, others, of whom Goldethorpe and Lockwood (1968) and Westergaard (1974) are possibly the most influential, have rejected such conclusions, implying that the thesis of embourgeoisement 'is based on assumption and not fact'. Westergaard (1974) wrote: 'The idea that the traditional English class structure has been steadily dissolved during the post-war period is one of the most pervasive and powerful of our contemporary myths.'

The lack of participation by working class people then may be a continuing phenomenon which has not been markedly eroded by the social changes associated with affluence and a longer exposure to education that has been characteristic of modern British society. This lack of involvement can have far reaching effects within the realm of leisure provision as Parry & Johnson (1975) illustrated: 'authorities use the criterion of maximum intensity of use as a justification for the investment of public money. Where facilities are provided but little used the expenditure is judged unjustifiable. In seeking maximum intensity of use, local authorities and the managers of facilities tend to seek continuity of usage by allowing bookings exclusively to clubs and organisations. This policy shuts out the casual user and also clashes with the criterion of 'openness' which is regarded as desirable where public provision is concerned'. Since working class people may be less likely to belong to organisations of this kind they can thus be discouraged from casual use of leisure facilities as individuals or families. Leisure provision thus becomes subject to middle class dominance. Curiously such a perpetuation of middle class values is not seen to be of particular concern to members of the Sports Council (e.g. Collins & Rees, 1975).

Earlier, Westergaard (1970) had clearly outlined the differences between the working class and middle class worker despite a levelling of wages. He wrote: 'his [the working class worker] is a distinctive subculture, conditioned and restricted by the cir-cumstances of working class life. The affluent worker is not turning 'bourgeois'. He does not aspire to assimilation in the middle classes and there are no signs in fact of such assimilation'. Bacon (1975) has shown how these differences operate in relation to leisure provision. He examined the interaction of working classes and middle classes or to be more specific 'the caretaking agencies' (his terminology) in the context of a new town. Bacon saw that the values of the caretaking classes appear to be evident throughout the whole area of leisure provision. The middle classes conceptualised successful leisure time in terms of attachment to, and formal participation in, organised clubs and associations. They were less appreciative of the informal, 'kin-based' patterns of interaction typical of traditional working class areas. Generally the local council was generous in its provision of lecture grants and financial support for all bodies which pursued such 'uplifting' aims. People engaged in such work, however, were unrepresentative of the general community. The caretaking agencies diagnosis of the working classes' lack of leisure participation appears to be couched in terms of 'surface' issues such as shiftworking, the problems caused by working mothers and the worker's lapse into passivity with beer and television. Bacon concluded that 'on balance the working class people would be leading less privatised lives if the public planning processes had become more democratically organised, were more flexible and responsive to the culture of the people they served, and if the consumers themselves had been given more real choice of control over detailed provision of local facilities and amenities'.

This explanation of the working classes' lack of participation within the leisure field can be referred to the use of 'spare' time being used for more work (Rapoport & Rapoport, 1974; Swades, 1958) either for pay or home improvements. On the other hand, Molyneux (1975) has shown concern about the continuing under-representation of the lower socio-economic groups in leisure pursuits: 'we are satisfied with our current state of ignorance on life styles, leisure habits and possible leisure aspirations of nearly half the population . . . we, the planners and administrators in local authorities remain in large part a middle class clientele catering in large part for a middle class clientele'.

Leisure, adolescents and society: contradictions

At a time when leisure facilities are available on a considerable (if not extensive) scale in Britain, it is pertinent to ask how far such leisure proposals represent preconceptions and value-judgements of those who are in positions of influence, clearly much discussion about leisure rests on the assumption that certain leisure pursuits are more rewarding and worthwhile than others.

The whole idea of planning for leisure may appear to be a contradiction in terms. Leisure is popularly regarded as 'free' time;

that area of an individual's existence where he can exercise choice about the use of his time as opposed to time spent at work or in school. Planning, on the other hand, implies an element of control—an invasion of personal freedom—not to the extent of telling people what they can and cannot do, but in the sense that choices will be limited to what is available or provided. In order to justify planning, Burton (1970) contended that 'if carried through successfully, it will provide a better overall provision of facilities for leisure'. But he begs the question—why should we be concerned with providing leisure facilities of particular kinds? The Scottish Standing Consultative Council on Youth and Community Service (1968) attempted to answer this question. 'Whatever the views held about leisure, there is general recognition that for individuals and communities its mode of use is an indicator as well as a powerful determinant of the quality of life they enjoy. Both socially acceptable and anti-social and delinquent uses of leisure depend to a large extent on the nature of opportunities also on the lack of them'.

Young people can be singled out for special attention in that they have particular needs associated with adolescence, and Leigh (1971) noted three main conditions which relate to their social lives and for which special provision ought to be made: lack of spending power requiring free or cheap provision, lack of transport requiring local provision, and exclusion by law or parental restriction from many of those meeting places which exist for adults.

In providing for the leisure of young people in the past, the aims of government were apparently to provide facilities to keep youngsters out of trouble rather than to provide the means for satisfying recreation (however defined) to improve the quality of life. There is no doubt that it was the anticipated social problems of the war and the fear of its effect on adolescent behaviour that prompted the creation of the Youth Service in 1939, to provide opportunities for young people to make use of their leisure. The report of the Albemarle Committee on the Youth Service (1960), which has sometimes been referred to as the 'Bible' of the youth service, did much to promote the needs of young people and the case for their special attention. However, Smith (1973) claimed that the interest came substantially out of the growing concern for rising rates of juvenile delinquency rather than a more positive viewpoint of providing for satisfying recreation, and that the state has only recently begun to find its way to a more forward-looking policy in leisure for youth. This dissatisfaction with provision for youth can be neatly summed up by quoting from Davies (1970). 'Youth work in Britain is in a state of thorough disarray . . . Many of the existing voluntary organisations, because they have such long histories, frequently display intense self-consciousness about their traditions and never fundamentally question their reasons for existing . . . The older teenager in particular, sensing that ultimate control lies with middle-aged and older adults, seems increasingly to display dissatisfaction by avoiding what youth establishments have to offer.'

If these criticisms were valid at the beginning of the 1970s, new proposals have since emerged. One of the sources for these ideas has been the Alexander Report (1975) which recommended the creation of the Community Education Service in its present form, combining youth work, community work and adult education. Its aims are as follows:

a. to promote learning as a lifelong activity so that people can acquire new knowledge and develop their individual talents and skills

b. to provide people with opportunities for continuous education irrespective of their age, sex, class, creed or status, enabling them to improve the quality of their lives both as individuals and as members of the community and, by releasing their will to work together, enabling them to contribute to the community education process themselves

c. to prepare people to participate fully in society and to offer them scope to predict and control those changes which result from their social and material progress

d. to implement the community education dimension of community development and, in so doing, to complement the provision for primary, secondary, further and higher education, and the provision for social work, recreation and other similar services.

It is important to remember that earlier provision was exclusively for youth whereas more recent provision refers to comprehensive provision, for lifelong education 'from the cradle to the grave'.

What is clear is that two main factors have historically influenced the expansion and contraction of youth and community service; firstly, a very real but vaguely defined fear of juvenile delinquency, and secondly, the economic situation. Commitment to the idea of youth and community service has never been complete and wholehearted. It has occupied a marginal position as a sort of luxury fringe to the education service. The emphasis there has been rather self consciously paternalistic, middle class and adult-dominated.

In studying youth and community centres, one of the models

which Eggleston (1976) found to be of major relevance was the 'socialisation model' in which the young are seen to be socialised or made ready for adult society—learning and accepting approved patterns of social behaviour, social structure, skills, knowledge and values. There are other models, but Eggleston noted 'the original and still dominant concern with socialisation'. With regard to organisations he found that statutory ones tended to be bureaucratic in their pattern of administration. Rather than participation, it was found that important decisions tended to be taken by full time officers. Tradition was seen to be an important element, determining current practice to a large extent. With regard to values, Eggleston felt that many of the changes introduced in recent years were more apparent than real. In almost all cases one of the main objectives of the organisation was that members should identify with their values. Eggleston felt that the predominant values that were being propagated were concerned with 'such matters as citizenship, the healthy way of life, the right mixture of competitions and co-operation, respect, loyalty and so on'.

Clearly not all young people will be attracted by such institutions, and the activities offered will not fit in with their general leisure styles. Eggleston's dominant model suggests conformity, acquiescence of approved patterns of behaviour, and little part to be played by adolescents in decision making. To paraphrase Sir John Maude's oft-quoted statement it is the aim of the youth service 'to offer individual young people in their leisure time, opportunities of various kinds . . . to discover and develop their personal resources of body, mind and spirit, and thus better to equip themselves to live the life of mature, creative and responsible members of a free society' (Albemarle Report, 1960). The Scottish Report on the Youth and Community Service (1968) added the enlightened phrase, 'and to derive enjoyment in the process'!

It is surprising how seldom enjoyment is considered, or even mentioned, as a criterion for measuring the success of leisure provision. This may be due in part to the widely held view that leisure is a compensatory activity—that since most people will end up in jobs which are dreary, monotonous and undemanding, with little opportunity for self-fulfilment, leisure can provide the satisfaction people need and becomes 'the sphere of life in which man may most fully realise himself, his hopes and his creative abilities' (Smith, Parker & Smith, 1973).

Whether due to conviction on the nature of leisure, or a basic reluctance to spend public money on young people 'having a good time', the aim of providing for enjoyment is rarely discussed. Perhaps there is a need to relate planning to research into the leisure patterns of young people, to provide what young people want, and enjoy doing, instead of providing what is supposed to be good for them.

Not surprisingly, one of the main areas of research has been on those young people who remain outside all forms of provision, to establish reason for their 'disassociation and disenchantment' in the hope of providing more suitable and attractive facilities for them. These are the young people West (1967) described as the 'unclubbable'—those who are often uninterested in or ineligible for the clubs and activities provided, or who have perhaps been removed from them because of their 'inappropriate' attitudes or behaviour. West suggested that for many, official youth activities are too tame or over-organised to appeal to them, and that it is from this hard core that delinquents are likely to be recruited. Society is thus likely to suffer. But just as important, the unattached youngster is also likely to suffer. In a study which aimed at describing the use made of youth service activities and assessing how far they met the needs of the young people for whom they were provided, Bone (1972) concluded that from most points of view, the youngsters who were 'unattached' to any club led less satisfactory lives than those who were 'attached'. Most of them were bored and unenthusiastic, were more timid, less socially apt and found making friends more difficult than the attached, and a smaller proportion of them claimed to be happy.

Until recently, this was the major area of concern in youth provision, since it was believed that the majority of young people were unattached. The unattached as Mobe (1970) has pointed out 'would scorn membership of any kind of organised Youth Service. But, far from spending their leisure time in any demonstrably constructive fashion, they were manifestly unhappy and frequently delinquent.

It is impossible to attract the unattached in any general way. Progress can only be made when one Youth Service worker is totally involved (incognito) with a small group, constantly, over a long period of time—and even this cannot be definitely attributed to the worker's efforts. Further, the communication methods employed are morally questionable'. The Albemarle Report (1960) suggested that only one in three youngsters made use of youth service provision, and nine years later, the figure of only twenty nine per cent was provided by the Youth Service Development Council's Report, 'Youth and Community Work in the 70s'. Bone's (1972) more exhaustive study, however, revealed that at a given time, sixty five per cent of young people are attached to a club. This much higher proportion is accounted for by the more comprehensive definition of 'club' which her survey employed, and which included all types of clubs or organisations associated with, or receiving assistance from, the youth service. Moreover, it was found that between the ages of 14 and 20, the proportion of young people in the sample who were, or had been, attached to a club for at least some period of time, rose to ninety three per cent—so only seven per cent of young people had never been attached. Equally, it is fair to state that many being 'disenchanted' are only briefly attached to clubs. Although the role of the 'detached' youth or social worker will still be important for this proportion of young people who remain inaccessible, Bone concluded that 'for the majority of the unattached, the main problem is one of increasing the attractions and value of organised groups for them before they become unattached. Not all studies have been quite so reassuring, however. Studying the leisure activities of 15–19 year olds in two areas of Glasgow and in a West Lothian mining town, Jephcott (1967) discovered that two out of three youngsters did not attend youth groups, and concluded that efforts to advertise would largely fail, since 'however persuasive the advertising, or energetic the push, plenty of youngsters will remain untouched, because with them the dimness of their leisure is one aspect of a generally deprived life'.

Although Scarlett's (1975) findings on the leisure patterns of Scottish youth have been criticised as being 'biased and superficial', and the sample can hardly claim to be representative of Scottish youth, there are some points of agreement with Jephcott's findings. One reason young people in both studies gave for not attending youth groups was that they were too closely linked with school, either because of the pattern of authority and discipline, or because school premises were used. In common with Jephcott, Scarlett found that a considerable proportion of leisure-time was not spent on any definite activity, and that youngsters often announced that they were bored. The most popular activity was found to be centred on the home, visiting or inviting friends, and this was also reported to be the most frequently mentioned pastime of young people by Bone's (1972) study of youth in England and Wales. All three studies noted that girls seem to be particularly poorly catered for and are less actively involved than boys in youth service activities.

It is clear from such evidence that much more may have to be done to encourage young people to use the facilities being provided for them, and equally those who supply the facilities should begin to approach young people to find out what is wanted and what would be attractive to them. However the Scottish Standing Consultative Council on Youth and Community Service (1968) actually warned against this and suggested that the natural effect of 'supply and demand' rarely produces well balanced provision. This danger was made apparent in Bone's study, which found that the young people who were attached to clubs showed greater interest than the unattached in having more facilities provided for them. This may mean that the unattached were largely satisfied with their less active lives, or more likely, that they were unable to think of ways in which their leisure lives could be improved. Besides, the evidence seems to suggest that supply very often creates demand— that 'people do not always know what they want to do until they actually try it' (Emmett, 1970). A study on indoor sports centres by the Sports Council (1971) reported that management policy, by programming certain activities during peak times of attendance, could significantly affect both the age range of the users of the centre and the balance between the sexes. The study also found that thirty per cent of participants had been introduced to an activity by the influence of the centres in their communities.

Emmett (1970) suggested therefore that the democratic aim of providing what people want is more often expanded into the utilitarian aim of ensuring the greatest happiness of the greatest number, by finding out what people would enjoy doing if they knew how and where to do it.

Linked to this is the paternalist aim of persuading people to do what is thought to be good for them, in the opinion of the suppliers of the facilities. Thus the widely prevalent view that 'sport is good for you' has resulted in an expansion in the provision of sports facilities. This argument is endorsed by Smith (1973) who maintained that the government, in a recent, more positive policy for leisure and youth, 'has generally found it easier to proceed on the firm ground of sport and physical recreation'. There has in fact been a dramatic rise in the number of modern, purpose-built sports centres in the country. Are sports centres the answer?

There is little doubt that participation in active sport is steadily rising. Burton (1970) reported that 'contrary to popular belief, organised team games are not losing participants at a rapid rate. On the other hand, many minority sports are attracting more and more adherents. Interest in sport is clearly widening as more "new" sports are discovered and more people take part in minority sports. There is no indication that interest in decreasing'. The Sports Council (1968) argued that while it might be true that some spectator sports were losing popularity, it was false to assume from this a decline in active participation. The report noted several indications of growth, particularly rising popularity of the more individual sports such as badminton, squash and golf, and concluded that the demand for sport was very strong and that only lack of facilities prevented further growth.

In the country's general provision for leisure then, sport and physical recreation seem to be receiving priority, and it is interesting to notice how this policy has been defended. On the one hand, there is the value-judgement, mentioned previously, about the benefit of sport to the individual. The Sports Council (1968) argued that physical recreation is able to provide challenging and satisfying leisure pursuits at a time when changes in the physical and mental demands of work have emphasised this need. Of course, this ignores the fact that people obtain satisfaction in different ways and that a sense of achievement, or physical challenge, or exertion may not fit into everyone's perception of satisfying and enjoyable leisure pursuits (despite potential health benefits). There is therefore little justification in the widely held assumption that activities involving positive physical effort are in some way 'better', and 'more worthwhile', than contemplative or passive ones. Although planners can excuse their actions by claiming only to meet a demand, it is clear that they have been influenced by the values attached to sport. Sports centres are extremely expensive to provide and to maintain, and few have tried to operate on a commercially viable basis. Atkin (1976) quoted one sports centre manager as admitting that prices for activities were high, but that they would have to be trebled if the centre was to 'break even'. Thus sports centres are expected to, and usually do, make enormous losses each year, and are subsidised heavily. Presumably they are not regarded as luxuries, as many critics suggest, but as valuable for their social and political benefits, 'where health, fitness and social morality have been the prime considerations . . . rather than unallayed enjoyment' (Burton, 1970).

The other argument for the provision of sports centres is that they form a vital part of community life. It is claimed that sport and physical recreation are essentially social activities, and that the main attraction for many people is the friendship and companionship found in them (Sports Council, 1968). Indoor sports centres are designed primarily to meet the leisure time needs of urban communities and are claimed by the Sports Council (1971) to be 'community sports halls, purpose-built and freely available for use by all sections of the general public'. It is true that they are purpose-built—but for sport rather than the community. The general secretary of the Central Council of Physical Recreation has said: 'These places need to be leisure centres, as opposed to sports centres. In the main, sports centres are austere, frightening, too big. It is this impersonality which is their greatest weakness' (quoted in Atkin, 1976). Taylor (1970) predicted that the programme of sports centre development would fail unless ordinary people with little or no sporting skill used these centres frequently, and that if centres became 'expensive clubs for experts', then sooner or later they would have to be closed, as constituting an unjustifiable expenditure of public money. In the current economic recession, sports centres have come under a great deal of localised pressure, since the bulk of their losses are underwritten by the local authorities. This has resulted in measures designed to cut losses, involving reductions in staff, fewer hours of opening and stiff price increases. However, the Minister for Sport warned that indiscriminate increases will deter the very people sports centres ought to be attracting, and claimed that one of the biggest mistakes had been the failure to link adequate social amenities to the facilities provided for sport (Atkin, 1976).

Although the sports centre claims to cater for the community, it is apparent that not all sections make use of its facilities. Despite their conclusion that the pioneering centres of the 1960s had set the pattern for 'what must be a very bright future', the Sports Council Study (1971) saw the need for more research in respect to design and management 'to ensure that the facilities are most effectively used by all ages and sections of the community', and in particular, to assess the attitudes towards sports centres of the working class population, who were vastly under-represented among centre users. In a break down of users in five sports centres into the Registrar-General's Social Classes the study found a marked skew in the distribution towards the upper end of the social class scale.

It is clear that sports centres are not the panacea many people expected them to be. Although the bulk of users are young people, it would be impossible to conclude from this that the leisure needs of young people are adequately met by sports facilities provision. Taylor (1970) pointed out that it is often believed that apathy can be removed by spending money on buildings and staff; that people can be induced to take part in sport and other activities if only facilities are available in a sufficiently attractive form and convenient location. But this totally ignores the factors surrounding consumer preference. Burton (1970) reported on American and British research which shows a relationship between the level of participation in sport and the level of income—high incomes are associated with high levels of participation in almost every sport. Although Scarlett (1975) recommended the lowering of costs (and many people advocate reducing prices instead of increasing them) to fill sports centres, evidence provided by Sillitoe (1969) makes it plain that the popularity of an activity often bears little connection with its relative cost—that apart from golf, cost differences do not account for the divergences in popularity of sports between socio-economic groups. Emmet (1970) has argued that other factors are more important: that such aspects as social class, sex, type of school attended and the teenage subculture influence a youngster's behaviour in many ways, and affect their view of the world which may or may not include certain activities. Emmett (1971) found that for many of the school-leavers in her sample, sport played a subordinate part in their lives.

Emmett used two guides to estimate the effect that social class has on attitudes to sport among school-leavers: the occupation of the father, as a measure of class origins; and the type of school attended, as a measure of the class it was likely the young person would ultimately achieve. Both measures produced the anticipated results—that young people who favoured sport were more commonly found among children with middle class values than among those with working class values. This trend was especially marked in the case of girls. The results of Emmett's study show that sport and physical recreation play a less important part in the lives of young people than is often assumed. Policy-makers are left in a very difficult situation, however, for even in Emmett's study, a reason commonly given by young people for not taking part in a sport is lack of suitable facilities. Other studies present the same problem for planners. Bone (1972) found that a relatively small percentage of youngsters in her sample mentioned active sport as a pastime, but in a question which asked what activities they would like to do if they had the chance, fifty eight per cent mentioned sport, the most frequently mentioned activity. Similarly, Sillitoe (1969) found that the most important reason given by both boys and girls having to give up activities in which they were interested when they left school was the lack of facilities. The comparison by Scarlett (1975) between Scottish and European youngsters did not support this, however, since she concluded that 'the distance of leisure facilities from the young people's homes and the general cost were roughly comparable from one country to another', yet young people on the Continent were more active than their Scottish counterparts. (It should be noted that this included activities in leisure facilities not wholly confined to sports.)

Planners are able to interpret such findings in two different ways—attempt to match the facilities for sport with the demand for them (which may be less than is often assumed), or provide the facilities on the basis that supply will create the demand (an effect which can occur but which varies in different sections of society and from sport to sport). Emmett pointed out that policy-makers could make use of her finding that boys are more actively interested in sport than girls, either by supplying fewer facilities for girls, or alternatively, by encouraging girls to make more use of the facilities. Ultimately the provision of sports facilities will depend on the values of the suppliers rather than the consumers. At the moment, the concensus of opinion favours the provision of sports facilities, so that young people who enjoy sport are relatively well catered for. But what about those who are less favourably inclined towards sport. What alternatives are offered?

Authorities have been at pains to justify the expenditure of public money in the provision for leisure for young people and while this has been relatively simple in the area of sport and physical recreation, it has been less easy to justify the existence of a youth club which may do little more than provide a meeting place for young people. The Albemarle Report (1960) stated that the youth service had to show that it provided opportunities for learning—'Learning is what the public will expect from the Youth Service, if they are to contribute to its cost'. Of course, few of the young people who make use of what the youth service has to offer ever think of it as an integral part of the education system—or would make use of it if they did! Most people interpret the educative role of the youth service in social terms, as preparing young people for their role as active members of the community. Smith (1973) criticised youth service provision on the grounds that it has been 'more concerned with amenity than community. It affords an occasion for meeting friends, for listening to pop music or playing games'. He went on to say that a compromise is needed between the expectations of members that their clubs are for fun with the more serious educational expectations of their leaders. The Youth Service Development Council (1969) justify youth service provision as achieving important purposes in the lives of young people—creating young people with wide, freely chosen interests, greater social confidence and poise, able to carry responsibility and who neither accept their society uncritically nor reject it totally. Nevertheless, such high ideals should not be allowed to obscure the basic need of young people, which the Report also stressed, to meet and mix in an informal and pleasant atmosphere.

Leisure time affords young people the opportunity to gain social experience, and the mere existence of a meeting place is often all that is required. Although Lady Albemarle is quoted as saying, 'They won't want to sit drinking coffee all the time'—even if they do, there may be a great deal of educative value in the social act. The need for young people to form happy, personal relationships was noted by the Newsom Report (1963) which drew attention to the existence of many less gifted young people who were 'socially maladroit' and who were often ill at ease even with their peers. Many of these young people resent being organised, and while most youth organisations would be intolerable for them (and probably intolerant of them), the provision of a club or centre which allows them to meet freely with a minimum of organisation and obligation may be the answer. Davies (1970) argued that the desire to do something, or participate in an activity, usually emerges out of a reasonably happy social situation, and that the provision made for young people will be most suitable and attractive where it has the reputation of being a happy place, 'where young people can meet each other and learn to find themselves and each other without being organised along ways they do not particularly want to go'.

Two key words which are frequently stressed in recent reports and studies involving youth provision are 'participation' and 'flexibility'. The Youth Service Development Council Report (1969) stated the overall purpose of the youth service as being 'the critical involvement of young people in a society which is theirs as well as ours', and the primary goal as the social education of young people. This may best be achieved by allowing them participation in the organising and administration of their own facilities. This is particularly true at a time when there seems to be a growing demand in all sectors of society for involvement in the decisions which affect their lives, and also at a time when young people seem less happy being told what to do. By participating in its management and organisation, young people could be enabled to shape provision to their needs. Provision should thus be flexible, allowing for local differences and resources, and responding to the particular needs of the individuals who use it. (Part of the problem with sports facilities is their inflexibility—both in terms of structure and management policy—and recent attempts to cater for 'non-sporting' interests, such as concerts or religious festivals, have been motivated by economic factors rather than an attempt to provide a wider based community centre, better able to attract a wide variety of youngsters.) Since it would be illogical to base provision entirely on the demands of young people—which can be expected to change with fashions—the most logical approach is to plan with flexibility in mind. Then the opinions, preference and attitudes of the young people who are participating in its management can be taken into account, and 'result in the modification of the initial plans in the light of emerging demands' (Scottish Standing Consultative Council on Youth and Community Service, 1968).

If we accept the premise that young people should be allowed to determine for themselves their own leisure provision, it appears that competitive commercial provision fulfils this condition. 'It was probably a waste of effort to provide costly, under used activities (for the older adolescent) when commercial provision was more flexible, more popular, and generally self-supporting' (Eggleston, 1976). This is often illusory, however, since commercial enterprises are only interested in providing for activities with wide profit margins, and to the extent that clubs or coffee bars achieve a virtual monopoly in any area, the young people have to accept what is offered with little opportunity for their own views to be taken into account. Besides, since commercial provision is usually costly, young people find it difficult to attend such places very often, and are forced to find other means of occupying their leisure. Despite the rising standards of living and the ever-widening range of activities being made available, there are still many people, especially among the young, who are bored.

Many of those who complain of boredom make very little effort to take part in any organised activity; and while it is obviously indefensible to force a person into doing something he does not want to do, society may have a responsibility to ensure that people should at least have a knowledge of what is available, so they can make an informed choice. Leigh (1971) considered the broad educational aim in relation to leisure is 'to increase both the true range of choices available, and the ability of the individual to make effective and significant choices'. Emmett (1970) argued that it is often very difficult for people to find out what facilities are available. Although commercial establishments are able to advertise widely to sell their facilities, it often appears that publicly provided facilities only communicate with the people who use them. Emmett postulated that 'everyone has better knowledge of commercial provision than they do of other provision; and articulate, pushing, middle class people with the right social networks are better able to find out about public provision and their rights in regard to publicly owned facilities than are less articulate people'. This may help in part to explain why high income groups use cheap and free facilities more often than do working class people.

Many young people then, just do not know what is available, but this is only one aspect of the problem of boredom. Even when they do know, they may be unwilling or unenthusiastic to make effective and satisfying choices. Bone's (1972) survey found that even among those young people who were 'attached' to clubs, the youngsters who attended youth clubs seemed to be least well off, were the most bored and unadventurous—although no less happy—compared with those who attended sports clubs and other clubs catering for specific interests. (It should be noted that these findings could give no indication of the mechanisms involved—whether youth clubs were the most successful in attracting the most bored and unadventurous, or whether they were least successful in improving these aspects of their members' lives). Scarlett (1975) also saw the need for more effective dissemination of information to young people, and argued that working class children are less likely to make 'constructive' use of available leisure opportunities than middle class children, since they have had less encouragement at home to teach them how to use their leisure. The solution she suggests is to give children education for leisure in school, where hopefully, 'being given a model in the formative years will help them to use opportunities which are available to them later'.

This is not a new idea, but one that was forcibly expressed in the Newsom Report which elaborated the role schools should take in leisure education, by encouraging the growth of extra-curricular activities as a part of school life, and using leisure activities in the curriculum. Children were to be presented with as wide a range of opportunities as possible, and encouraged to try a wide variety of activities. Leigh (1971) would argue, however, that the emphasis in schools has tended to concentrate on education through leisure rather than for leisure—activities have been seen as means to achieving personal and social development, and little attention has been paid to the future and to ensure that leisure becomes 'the source of enjoyment and benefit it ought to be, and not of demoralising boredom' (Newsom Report, 1963).

Membership of school clubs, societies or organisations is not part of the common, accepted experience of young people in secondary schools. It is probably an experience which is more common among the more able, rather than the average or less able, pupils and it is probably also for the more able groups that most opportunities exist. At least half of those who leave school at fifteen have no opportunities at all of this kind and therefore actual experience among this group may be very limited indeed . . .

It is dangerous to assume that those who do take part in school clubs and societies necessarily participate very much either in the practical organisation of the activity with which they are concerned or in the social organisation of the group with which they are involved . . . There is little evidence that conscious efforts are made in schools to teach pupils the skills of social organisation nor, in general, that teachers regard it as any part of their job to provide such teaching . . .

Although there are certain privileged minorities, prefects, sixth formers, and sports teams' captains, for example, who are willingly or unwillingly thrust into leadership positions where they may haphazardly learn the skills of social organisation we cannot assume that the majority of young people at present leaving our schools have had experiences which are in any way helpful to them in this respect' (Leigh, 1971).

Findings by Bone (1972) which showed that pupils who stay on at school beyond the minimum leaving age tended to have led a more varied leisure life than those who left school at the minimum age, support this point of view.

Despite the efforts of the school, it seems likely that many children adopt the life style of their parents and peers, and that children from socially deprived areas thus arbitrarily cut down their choice of leisure pursuits. Also, in the sense that school is often an unpleasant experience for such children, the link between school and leisure may serve to narrow, rather than widen, the leisure opportunities available.

The identity of youth as a distinct 'subculture' has perhaps tended to obscure their needs as individuals, and as leisure is essentially personal (although the individual may be influenced by such factors as social class, peers and parental attitudes), the recreational activity he chooses should be what he (legitimately) wants, not necessarily what society wants him to have. When society provides facilities, the provision is inevitably influenced by value-judgements about the nature of leisure and recreation. While there exists a considerable proportion of young people who are bored, and who spend most of their free time doing nothing in particular, serious doubts must be raised not only about the adequacy of the present provision but to the relevance of the value-judgements behind it. A variety of facilities and activities would be the most acceptable form of provision, where young people have freedom to choose not only the activity they want, but the way they want to enjoy the activity. The essence of satisfactory leisure is not simply the freedom to choose, but to choose something enjoyable. Further the likelihood is that choice though individualised will also reflect subcultural life styles.

What are present-day adolescents like?

Local authority provisions usually include such facilities as libraries, museums, art galleries, exhibition and drama centres, as well as parks with open spaces for cricket, tennis, bowling and putting. Educational establishments provide a range of sporting facilities, evening classes and community areas. Voluntary organisations (often originally church initiated) offer further facilities. All three have a strongly traditional approach and are slow to change. Closer to the values and needs of the individual user is the variety of facilities provided by privately organised clubs—individuals who together formed a group in order to preserve resources for their own specialist needs in leisure. They tend to be middle class dominated. The power to change and to meet the needs of the members is within the hands of the members—thus the clubs can be more flexible to change than traditional facilities generally offered by public authorities. In this type of club Sillitoe (1969), for example, found that there was more participation in activities such as table tennis, fencing, archery, shooting, badminton, squash, tenpin bowling, dancing, golf and cricket than in authority premises offering the same activities.

More flexible still and less bound by traditional values is the commercial leisure industry. The values which set limits to their provision for leisure are based on maintenance of sufficiently wide profit margins and that they are still within the bounds of legality for continued existence. Thus they can cater for latest fads in leisure demands. But at the same time, because of cost, many young people are excluded. Thus the cheap, or free facilities provided by authorities tend to be based on certain traditional values of the planner.

But what determines what young people want in leisure? We have already noted the influence of social class in this area (see pp. 102–4) but Emmett (1970) has argued that there are other factors involved; the type of school attended and 'teenage subcultures' to which the adolescent is exposed. Emmett also argued that early socialisation patterns are important. Patterns by which the child is inculcated with the values of the adult world—in particular his 'significant others'—have a profound effect on later choices.

Bernstein (1961) in his study of language codes pointed to different codes of socialisation of the young child in the middle class and working class families. Not only are there differences in use of language but in methods of child control and socialisation. Not only the patterns, traditions, habits and values of a subculture or family but the quality of life enjoyed there can be carried into leisure activities and thus affect choice of activity.

It is important, therefore, to try to discover what the majority of teenagers are really like, since Smith (1973) has suggested that the overwhelming majority of adolescents continue the traditions—in work, marriage, childrearing and in leisure—of the society in which they grow up. The idea of a teenage generation which has rejected the values of its parents for a mixture of violence and lethargy, is revealed as totally unrealistic in a report on Britain's 16-year olds (Fogelman, 1976). Teenagers emerged as thoroughly traditional. They had a firm belief in marriage and the family and a marked desire, both in their present lives and in plans for their careers, to find ways of helping others. They get on well with their parents and even their teachers reported surprisingly few cases of bad behaviour. Yet it was clear that teenagers' lives are not without difficulties. The researchers asked no questions about use of drugs or experience of sex, as answers were expected to be evasive. But drink was confirmed as a problem; and so was truancy. School was seen as an imposition by large numbers.

Even though the teenagers admitted they quarrelled fairly frequently with brothers and sisters many said this 'did not mean there was anything wrong with the underlying relationship'. Dress and hairstyle were the main causes of friction between parents and children. Next in this 'league' was trouble over times of coming in at night or going to bed. Doing homework and choice of friends of the same sex led to rather fewer disputes.

Watching television was the leading recreation, with two-thirds watching 'often'. Only one in twenty claimed to watch it 'never or hardly ever', compared to one in four who 'never or hardly ever' read a book. 'Fortunately,' the report added, 'the proportions dancing or taking part in sporting activities indicate that life is not altogether sedentary.' Most went out only about once or twice a week, but fifteen per cent went out five times or more. Almost half had had an alcoholic drink in the week before the survey and about a fifth said they had been into a public house for a drink, even though this was illegal.

A large percentage thought school was largely a waste of time and found homework a bore. Teachers estimated that only eight per cent were regular truants; but fifty two per cent of the teenagers said they had stayed away at some time or other. Reasons for occasional absence included helping at home and wanting to do 'something special' away from school, but twenty per cent said they had stayed away because they were 'fed up with school'. Scarlett (1975) has commented on the obvious need to 'ensure that so-called "non-academic" pupils receive teaching and training according to their particular abilities which may be more relevant to their future lives'.

A report of Scottish teenagers revealed a rather similar pattern (Scarlett, 1975). Whilst up to the age of about fourteen years most Scottish youngsters in Scarlett's sample were involved with their families and tended to stay at home most of the time, after this there was a breakaway from the family unit. Yet there was no real evidence of a serious rift in family relationships. Most families seemed to have worked out a system of independence to a degree for young people, who seemed to be given most of the freedom they wanted.

At school Scottish youngsters were not treated sufficiently like adults from their viewpoint; this seemed to have two results. On the one hand it produced a backlash on the part of youngsters in the shape of negative attitudes to school, and on the other hand their initiative seemed stifled because of the paternalistic system that discouraged independent action.

A number of youngsters complained about the lack of places to go where they could meet other young people, about the lack of alternatives to discotheques, and about the general lack of opportunity for adventure in their lives. Their leisure patterns were predictable enough: visiting friends in their own homes and having friends around appeared to be the most popular activity of Scottish youngsters. Television, pop music, listening to records, going to pubs (under age or otherwise), the cinema, discotheques and dancing were also vitally important.

The report commented that it seemed to be hardly surprising that Scottish youngsters used alcohol regularly, given the example of adults which is very much an alcohol consuming model. In some cases the national character may be involved. A seventeen year old boy from Glasgow explained 'You cannae chat up a bird if you ha'nae had a drink. We take about six or seven shorts before going to the dancing just enough to let us in so that we are not drunk, but it takes effect afterwards. After a while you realise like me, that I'm seventeen and on the road to alcoholism. It's just terrible'.

The findings of Scarlett and Fogelman discredit to some extent any theory of a generation gap. Young people today appear to accept adult models in their social environment and develop life styles commensurate with the values of their subcultural background and upbringing. Nevertheless there are certain signs of change in many facets of society, and these may be particularly apparent in leisure life-styles and the differing value structures of subcultural groupings of adolescents. The next chapter examines their leisure pursuits, including sports, and traces the influence of family background and social influences on their leisure patterns.

CHAPTER 8

Young people and leisure life-styles

In the previous chapter it was suggested that public leisure provision is, to a large extent, offered to young people under certain conditions which may deter their wholehearted involvement. Yet adolescence is for a number of reasons a peak of leisure involvement. How young people resolve this dilemma, and their variety of leisure pursuits—legal and delinquent—provide a number of insights into the interests and values of particular subcultures in our society.

In studying such patterns it seems natural to begin with the family, and their influence on life-styles and sports participation.

Family sports environment

The importance of the family in establishing children's general life-styles, attitudes to the educational system and sports has meant that educational research has until recently tended to focus on the home rather than on the school. Fraser's (1959) study identified the most important factor determining a child's progress at school as 'parental encouragement'. Douglas (1964), Wiseman (1964), Mays (1965), Douglas, Ross & Simpson (1968) also investigated the relationship between home and school and found similar results. Klein (1965) suggested that the casual relationships between socio-economic variables and attainment might be due to subcultural differences in children's levels of aspirations and in their ability to postpone gratification. These dispositions, it was argued, may have their origin in the distinctive child-rearing and socialisation practices of different social groups.

The family then is a potent force in motivation, academic success and attitudes to schooling, sex roles and the development of physical abilities. Movement skills and attitudes acquired in the family may reinforce dispositions towards sports participation and evaluation of specific physical activities. This in turn, can lead to interest and performance in physical activities by the individual. In a general sense the influence of the family can range from the function of movement in the process of socialisation into physical activity to the more specific induction of children into particular activities by interested family members.

In the United States Orlick (1972) has indicated that any 'average' child placed in a very positive family sports environment will almost surely be an early participant in sports regardless of other factors. In several cases brothers described as complete opposites in terms of personality, level of activity, size, ability, were either both participants or both non-participants in sports, depending upon their family sports environment. Once a child does become an early sports participant, whether or not he continues becomes largely dependent upon the positive and negative reinforcements operating in the organised sport environment, as well as in the home. Parents of children who elected to participate in sport were found to provide both a model of participation and positive reinforcement for sports behaviour (as evidenced by their own participation, their viewing habits, their expectations regarding their child's participation, and their encouragement for their child's participation).

On the other hand, fear of failure, or the psychological stress of disapproval, appeared to influence certain children to the extent that they were afraid to participate (Orlick, 1972). Eighty per cent of the mothers interviewed by him expressed a strong dislike for the emphasis on winning and the competitiveness in children's sports. They thought the emphasis should be put on fun and enjoyment, along with giving each child an equal opportunity to play. As far as sport is concerned, this cultural transmission is supported in a British investigation by Crunden (1970). He found that the children under investigation did not avail themselves equally of the opportunities which existed for participation in sport, and these differences could be stratified in relation to sex and family background.

Adolescent socialisation. At adolescence the process of socialisation still operates but the importance of the different forces changes. Adolescent roles and peer groups become more important in determining physical activity interests and influencing behaviour.

In British society adolescent males are considerably more physical-activity loving than girls and every investigation of this topic emphasises this difference. Jephcott (1967) in a study of how

Glasgow teenagers spend their leisure time concluded that sport, (mainly in the form of scratch football), was a common interest among boys, but attracted little attention from girls. The Schools Council enquiry into school leavers (Morton-Williams & Finch, 1968), showed that to well over a third of the boys sport was important but to only a sixth of the girls. Mating and consideration of attractiveness seem important to a girl's adolescent role in western society and most physical activity does not appear to be recognised as enhancing these elements of the girl's self-image and status. Aggressiveness and physical skill are compatible with a boy's search for identity and acceptance, but refinement and pleasing appearance are part of the girl's role which does not appear to them to be promoted by most physical activities. Changes in women's role in society may over time create changes in attitudes and characteristics, and these in turn may well be reflected in the future sporting pursuits of women. My own prediction is that certain groups of women will engage more and more in 'masculine' sports.

The peer group is a further important influence in determining the role expectation of adolescents. There appears to be a natural expansion from family relationship to affiliation into groups or gangs, although Cohen (1956) showed that there are subcultural differences and that urban working class adolescents are most likely to develop group allegiances.

For many adolescents the work they do at school is neither interesting nor rewarding. 'The majority of secondary school pupils are from working class homes and are destined for manual employment. They are . . . placed in a contradictory situation, being socialised into assumptions and responses appropriate to a middle class career while at the same time being excluded from the rewards of this system. The middle class pupils are . . . offered a career but at the price of a certain lopsidedness in their personal development . . . they are expected to consistently improve their level of intellectual performance, while at the same time sublimating their emotional and sexual capacities and channelling their creativity into channels approved by the school . . . They are therefore faced with the problem of retrieving these expressive areas of experience. Due to the very low level of control which pupils possess over the structure of their school situation, these contradictions must be resolved in the sphere of non-work and leisure'. Thus Murdock and Phelps (1973) summarised the contradictions contained in the school or work situation which result in the formation of a leisure-based subculture. It would, however, be a mistake to see particular youth subcultures as entirely determined by social class. Once formed, they assume a certain degree of autonomy, and influence in turn the rules and meanings of adolescent life styles.

Milson (1972) has offered a useful typology for considering adolescents, their life-styles and leisure patterns 'through their own eyes'. 'Conformists' represent the majority of young people who will absorb the dominant values of society (e.g. Fogelman, 1976); 'experimenters' who can be either political revolutionaries or personal revolutionaries devising a life style which allows them to opt out for some time and in some way from the achieving society; and the 'deprived socially rejected and desocialised' who comprise the delinquent, the disgruntled, the 'drifters' and who do not fit into society.

Adolescent subcultures and sports participation. Coleman's (1961) study of American schools examined the 'climate of values' of adolescent subcultures, and he found that few leisure activities had any relation to pursuits which go on in school. 'Some of the hobbies may, of course, have their genesis in school, and some sports are centred around the school, but, except for these, school activities are missing.' School may play an even less central role in the life of the British adolescent: 'The social life of the adolescent in school may have from the teenager's perspective, a definite old-fashioned air. Some also want the sort of activities provided by commercial enterprises but for which the school is generally un-willing to cater' (Hargreaves, 1972).

Furthermore, in a sample of early leavers, Hendry (1976) found that the number of male sports participants decreased more than fourfold after leaving school and that of females by almost six.

Hence a framework of analysis can be postulated, which states that success, praise and identity within the school can lead to a commitment to sports by certain pupils and this reinforces further participation out of school. Pupils who reject or experience rejection within school are less likely to be involved in leisure sports and turn to a 'pop' based culture (Sugarman, 1967). Inherent theories of play do not explain non-participation, but by con-sidering social reinforcers an explanation is possible. Some pupils may experience effects in the activities themselves, which are either pleasurable or otherwise—painful physical contact for instance—but more importantly perhaps are the social influences experienced by pupils within school sports. For these alienated pupils other social agencies reinforce alternative behaviours which orientate them towards a teenage culture centred around the peer group. There are many sources of positive and negative reinforcement within the school and social environment which continue to project pupils towards particular and different interests and involvements.

The very attraction of leisure pursuits seems to be grounded in the peer group. In Hendry's studies (1975, 1976) boys who did not participate in sport often indicated an interest in cycles, motorcycles, and cars; mildly aggressive rough and tumble games; or just 'hanging about' with a group of friends in their leisure time. Obviously these activities are less culturally approved for girls, and other pursuits such as dancing, dating, meeting friends for coffee, listening to records, seemed to satisfy their need for social contact. Pop music and discotheques, as Murdock and Phelps (1973) have outlined, are in many ways central elements in adolescent leisure, particularly for girls, from which many subsidiary activities flow. Indeed there appears to be some antipathy between pop culture and sport as Emmett (1971) has shown with secondary school pupils.

Yet physical activities are important in some adolescent group structures. It is possible that as well as providing the opportunity for acquiring some of the skills necessary for living in a society, the peer group, as Thrasher (1936)·claimed, provides opportunities for excitement and adventure not possible in society generally, and in such a climate prowess in physical skills may be desirable. For example, Jephcott's (1967) study of adolescent activities shows amongst other things, the greater significance of dancing, cinema-going, and cafe visiting than sports for both boys and girls, and in the sporting interests of boys the overwhelming pull of 'scratch football'. Emmett (1971) revealed very interesting variations in involvement in various kinds of physical activity according to age, social class, type of school, degree of involvement in the pop culture, and solitariness. In Finland Helanko (1957) demonstrated a relationship between interest in team games and a particular stage of social development. He identified four periods of social development. Before the age of nine children associated in loose aggregations, the period from nine to twelve years is marked by a strong gang phase, the period twelve to sixteen marked by a looser gang stage during which individuals or small groups drift away from the gang to take up other activities, and the period after the age of sixteen is marked by a second stage of aggregation when adolescents come together as individuals or groups of two or three in common meeting places. His investigation into involvement in sports showed that even when a sports club was a centre for the aggregation of older adolescents, one half did not participate in sports, and only one quarter claimed sports as a major interest.

Leigh's (1971) study also painted an interesting picture of the adolescents' stereotyped recreational life, in which active and outdoor pursuits were of minimal importance. For the typical member of the sample, leisure was a progression from home to pub, club, an occasional dance and perhaps a football match (as a spectator) on Saturdays. The author made no systematic attempt to measure participation in physically active recreation, but in the total sample there were only a score of memberships of sporting clubs, chiefly football and fishing. Informal social visiting was much more important (especially for purpose of 'courting'). The vast majority of non-participants in Hendry's (1975) investigation indicated that they were seldom bored with these spare-time interests—indeed an important reason for not following sports was because of other interests and involvements. Active adolescents also involved themselves in non-sporting pursuits which enabled them to meet their friends and socialise outside the home. The interesting point, however, was their dual leisure involvement aligning them to their peers, and centring round common interests and pop music. So in leisure sports participants perhaps show a greater range in their social relations than non-participants, with a greater opportunity to experience a wider selection of social roles.

Most British studies have emphasised the important relationship between social class and participation in physical activities both in secondary schools (only a quarter of children in low social class groups had a keen interest in sports compared with almost half of those in the high social classes (Emmett, 1971) and in adult life (Sillitoe, 1969). Hendry's study also showed that a non-manual social class was related to sports involvement both in school and in leisure time.

A further study by Hendry and Simpson (1977) on regular users of a sports and community centre revealed a similar pattern in terms of leisure pursuits and differing life-styles. In this single, purpose-built sports and community centre, two distinct and separate subcultures existed. There was little, or no, rapport between the two groups of members. Sports members were content to stay in the sports area and apparently saw nothing to attract them to the community area. Although the two groups remained isolated in this way, a middle group of young people did exist which frequented both areas. By the time they reach the age of fourteen years, however, most of this dual membership group will have opted for one area or the other. It appears to be a largely one-way movement to the community area. This would seem to contradict Scarlett's (1975) suggestion that one of the reasons for non-participation in 'constructive' leisure pursuits is a lack of information, since community members appear to have ample knowledge about what is available to them in the sports area and reject it.

Two questions arise. Firstly, where do most of the sports

members come from, if not from the dual membership group? Secondly, why do most of the dual membership group choose the community area rather than the sports area? The first can be readily answered from the results of the study. The majority of sports area members came from a wider radius than the community members, and attended to take part in specific activities for which the centre catered. The dual membership group thus appears to be 'local kids' who enjoy doing anything that is being offered, but when they outgrow this youthful vitality they tend to adopt the values of local adolescents, the majority of whom are largely anti-sports area.

This brings us to the second question. Why do the majority of young people in the neighbourhood of the centre choose not to attend the sports area? One possible reason which suggests itself is costs, but there was little evidence of a shortage of money in the community area, judging from the sales at the coffee bar counter and the extremely high incidence of smokers among members.

Many of the community members, particularly the boys, complained that there were too many rules in the sports area, and that it was too strict. The results showed that an overwhelming majority of the sample in the community area regarded sports area leaders as being strict and unsympathetic, and a substantial proportion felt they interfered too much. Surprisingly perhaps, they agreed with the necessity of rules and tight discipline in a sports hall (mainly for the prevention of accidents and damage to equipment) and were not therefore advocating a sports area without rules. Instead, rather than subject themselves to the discipline and the rules, they preferred not to attend.

The findings by Jephcott (1967) that many youngsters do not attend activities because they are too closely linked with school— either because of the pattern of discipline, or because school buildings are used—seemed to fit the sports area under study. As the results showed, community members in general did not accept school values to any great extent, most of them leaving school early, and few being involved in school activities, so any linkage of the school with the sports area would tend to make the sports area less attractive for them. Girls, in particular, presented age as a reason for not taking part in sports area activities, and a common explanation was that, 'you get too old for jumping about like that'. Several of the girls who were interviewed had been members of the gymnastics club, one of the most popular activities in the sports area, but felt that they were too old 'to make fools of themselves' any longer. The girls in question were only fifteen and sixteen years of age.

Regular attenders at the sports area who were 'serious' users of the facilities were easily identifiable by their 'uniforms' of tracksuits, specialised clothing and equipment, and often identical sports bags. Clearly subcultures exist which do not accept the values of sport. Girls, for example, dressed and behaved in a way obviously meant to attract the male members of the community area, and many admitted to attending only with this in mind. In such cases, sport does not fit into the picture at all.

The study was further concerned with attempting to answer the basic question, are the two groups of young people different and have they chosen quite different leisure styles? The results showed quite clearly that the two subcultures were very different. Differences were such that many members could see them for themselves: 'It's the brainy ones who go to the sports area, the ones here are all mental', remarked a seventeen year old girl in the community area.

Aspirations were also very different. Evidence from studies such as the sports Council (1971) has suggested that sports centres are predominantly middle class havens with few working class users. What the present results showed was that sports members tended to be middle class aspirants. The majority of them chose non-manual occupations, a considerable proportion of which were professional, most notably teaching. Community members were more likely to choose manual occupations, the boys choosing trades while the girls chose mainly office work of some description. Community members maintained that the young people in the sports area were snobs, and though impossible to substantiate, what is important is that they perceived a difference between themselves and those in the other group. By contrast, fewer sports members were able to suggest differences of such a kind between the groups and most claimed to know none of the community area users on which they could base an opinion. One fourteen year old girl who *did* have an opinion, and who was completely frank, declared confidently that sports members were more sensible and intelligent and that community members were 'rough, always swearing, smoking, fighting and getting into trouble'.

It is clear that not all children consider sport as part of their school or leisure life, and as this study suggests mere encouragement will not necessarily produce more sport-loving people. The two groups proved to be different in their attitudes towards the centre, and what they expected to get out of it. For sports members, attendance at the centre was for one reason—to take part in activities they enjoyed. To do this, they were willing to travel fairly long distances and spend considerable sums of money on transport, so presumably considered the effort worthwhile. A fourteen year old girl in the sports area spent over £1 each week on bus fares, but considered it better spent that way than sitting in a coffee bar.

Community members were less united in their motives for attending the community area, enjoyment of activities being only one reason. For most of them it was a place for meeting and talking with their friends, not to meet new friends but to continue their established friendship patterns in a relaxed, fairly comfortable, cheap and convenient manner. The results confirmed that for many of them, especially the girls, the centre was only somewhere to go, since they had nothing else to do. One boy said 'I come here to get out of the house', others unenthusiastically claimed, 'It's better than sitting at home'. Complaints and criticisms seemed to be part of their 'enjoyment' of the centre and it was observed that every member who was interviewed in the community area had at least one unfavourable comment to make about it. For example, two girls admitted they only attended for 'the talent' but complained that the talent was hopeless!

Coupled with complaints were pleas for more organised activities, especially among the girls who felt neglected (cf. Bone, 1972). Yet when asked to be more explicit, they were unable to say exactly what they wanted. This seemed to be an important difference between the two groups—the sports members knew what they wanted, and made an effort to achieve their desires, whereas community members were often unable to say what they wanted or to communicate their needs, and made little effort to change things.

Sport is only one way a young person can occupy his leisure time and the need for sport does not exist in equal amounts in all young people. Indeed, in some it does not exist at all. The need to meet and form relationships with other young people is however a generally felt need, and sport is only one (perhaps not very satisfactory) way of fulfilling this desire. In their attitudes towards the centre, it was clear that for community members, the centre was the hub of their leisure time, around which their leisure lives revolved. For most of sports members, the centre was only one of the places they attended where they met like-minded young people engaged in the same kind of activity. In effect, the centre provides a meeting place for two separate subcultures—a community area which is used by the local young people, and a sports area which is patronised by a wider based, sports loving community. In their leisure time spent outside the centre the pattern of commercial leisure involvement of both groups was somewhat similar, with disco dancing, casual swimming, ice rink skating, tenpin bowling, cinema and theatre going, attendance at football matches and public houses being mentioned. Yet in their membership of youth organisations and participation in sports teams not connected with school there were considerable differences: forty two per cent of male sports members and twenty three per cent of girls belonged to youth organisations by comparison with five per cent of community area boys and thirteen per cent of community girls. Fifty two per cent of sports area boys, forty one per cent of sports area girls played for sports teams whereas only twenty eight per cent of community area boys and thirteen per cent of girls played for teams. At this stage it is perhaps necessary to turn our attention to less clearly observable aspects of adolescent leisure.

Life-styles and delinquency

Definitions of delinquency normally stress two aspects of the delinquent act: that it is illegal and that it is committed by children or adolescents. A delinquent act is therefore distinguished from a deviant act which may violate society's norms of conduct but which is not deemed illegal. Official statistics may not represent the actual incidence or distribution of delinquent behaviour because procedures for arrest may change, because there may be a social class bias in law enforcement and because only a small fraction of offences is detected. Delinquency can be the result of constitutional factors and/or environmental factors. Theoretical approaches to delinquency can be crudely classified into those which are individually centred and those which are socially centred. An even cruder dichotomy is to suggest that psychologists tend to use the first approach and sociologists the second. An individual behaviourist approach, for example, is that of Eysenck (1964) who has related delinquency to poor conditionability. Other traits listed as criminogenic by Eysenck include psychomotor clumsiness, and emotional instability, when combined with extraversion and a mesomorphic physique.

Social approaches suggest the impact of social learning including both peer and adult behavioural models. The boy who has made no headway among his more respectable peers can gain status by acts of aggression, theft and vandalism. Or if a 'criminal community' flourishes in the neighbourhood some children will more easily learn the criminal role; in the more socially alienated slums delinquency remains unsophisticated and impulsive as part of the subculture. Matza (1964) argued that the stereotype of the delinquent as a person committed to an oppositional culture does not ring true for most delinquents when they are actually met or spoken to. Why do they cease to offend when they become older? Matza believes that delinquents evade rather than oppose the dominant morality and do this by selecting and extending trends that exist in the wider culture.

Thus one cannot discount the possibility that crime and delinquency in our society are in some measure the cost of certain kinds of social development. This is Wilson's (1966) thesis. As a reaction against the growing institutionalisation of daily life in society—mass education and mass entertainment—some people turn to delinquent patterns of behaviour in search of personal identity. These are the people who 'live for kicks'. Wilson also argued that the predominant ethic of our society is acquisitiveness and desire for success. These values are transmitted to the population by the mass media, but unfortunately not everyone can be rich or successful. Some who never become either feel that they have been cheated, and become delinquents or criminals.

In arguing about boredom and delinquency Miller (1966) stated that all the psychological advantages went to the boy or girl (usually with academic interests) who is able to stay at school until later adolescence. He pointed out that among many aetiological reasons for the disturbance of youth would appear to be the inability to use leisure. For many adolescents there is both too much leisure and too few usable resources, both inside the personality of the individual and in the surrounding environment, for free time to be enjoyable.

Brooke Taylor (1970) has written that it is time to question the basic assumptions that have long been made about the uses of leisure. When people say that one leisure activity is more 'rewarding', 'useful', or 'creative' than another, what are the assumptions on which they base their judgment? The first assumption uncovered by Brooke Taylor is the one that active leisure pursuits are better than passive ones; most British schools require their pupils to take part in some form of sporting activity. As we have seen earlier, sport is only one form of leisure activity and it is an activity which in its organised forms does not appeal to all adolescents. Yet Patrick (1970) has shown that sport and delinquency are not necessarily antipathetic: 'Most of the gang were members of the local Youth Club which they attended two or three times a week. In addition, 'scratch' games of football were arranged for Saturday and Sunday afternoons in the near-by municipal park or in the playground of the local school. Trouble as Jephcott (1967) styled it, began after the Club was closed, and the football match was played. As McKay (1959) wrote,

"Organised recreation and delinquency are not mutually exclusive activities".' McKay (1959) argued that participation in organised recreation represents such a small proportion of the total life experience of the adolescent: 'to suggest that a boy will not be delinquent because he plays ball is no more valid than to say that he will not play ball because he is delinquent. He may do either, neither, or both'. He did admit, however, that the fact that organised recreation does not eliminate delinquency does not detract from its value in any way—it is just that it is a mistake to justify recreation in terms of preventing delinquency. McKay has compared delinquency and other forms of recreation claiming that they have many qualities in common. 'In its early stages, delinquency is clearly a form of play. It is easy to see that running away from home, stealing pies from a pie wagon, or driving a stolen car may satisfy some of the basic needs and desires that are satisfied conventionally by base-ball, pleasure riding or going on a camping trip. In fact it is easy to see that for those involved in them, many forms of delinquency, though costly to the community, may satisfy more of the immediate needs and wishes of children than are satisfied by more conventional forms of recreation. And this competition between the two types of activity is further complicated if the delinquency becomes financially profitable.' Other writers have pointed out that the values underlying juvenile delinquency are far less deviant than is commonly portrayed. According to Matza and Sykes (1961) there is a close parallel between the juvenile delinquent and the gentleman of leisure, who has a disdain for work, identifies masculinity with tough, aggressive behaviour and is constantly in search of thrills and adventures.

On the other hand, Yablonsky (1959) studied gangs in New York, many of which spring up for the sole purpose of criminal activity. The vast majority of the groups he studied were loosely structured, composed of unhappy and disturbed children involved in serious forms of delinquency. It was the gangs' very lack of organisation and absence of expectations that constituted its primary sources of satisfaction; he found that youths affiliate with a gang not for a feeling of belonging and solidarity, but because it is an organisation within which they can relate to others in spite of their limited social abilities. These gangs had a shifting membership, with usually seven to eight core members and twenty to twenty-five 'peripherals', the leaders being severely emotionally disturbed. This ties in well with the picture of Glasgow gangs (Patrick, 1970). It was this very looseness of structure that enabled Patrick to join a gang (as a 'peripheral') and his subsequent work as a participant observer throws light on the life of a gang. He found that group cohesion was low, and interpersonal relationships were shallow and superficial: he agreed with Yablonsky's picture of the core psychopath, whose prowess in violence could terrify the followers. At the same time, Patrick portrayed the leader as 'a socially ineffectual youth incapable of transferring leadership ability and functioning to more demanding social groups'.

Further, one senior gang in the district commanded the allegiance of most of the smaller and younger gangs. Many of the active gang members were still schoolboys. Part of the enjoyment in the gang setting was excitement and aggression. One 'colleague' of Patrick, who, on describing his most exciting moments as being those just before a big fight said 'Yer hert's racin', yer knees get weak—it's better'n sex!' Patrick's fellow gang members realised that they were educational, social and occupational failures, well and truly 'at the bottom of the heap'; the deep frustrations they experienced as a result gave rise to aggression which had to have an outlet.

Disillusionment had set in during school days, as Patrick realised: 'Tim's considered opinion of his school-days was "Aw Ah ever goat wis techey (technical) drawin"'.' Together with other core members of the gang, he had been in Class 2DF which they explained in a matter-of-fact way as 'the daft class'. Tim's attitude to education had not always been negative. He remembered being keen on school work at the beginning of his secondary school career. He had started his homework one night amidst the mockery of elder brothers. Finally, one of them had become so riled at his persistence that he had thrown the school-books into the fire. The following day Tim again excused himself by asserting that he had lost his books. Never again did he attempt to do any homework. All the boys I met were withering in their scorn and hatred of their schools and for the external trappings of education—uniforms, school bags, books'.

Miller (1966) has written that little danger exists for academic adolescents because they do not experience long periods of available leisure time. But non-academic adolescents have too much leisure and 'too few usable resources'. An illustration of this is the fact that up and down the country bored young people sit in coffee bars waiting for someone to suggest an activity, legal or illegal. Miller suggested the establishment of a differential working week, with sixty hours being the norm for a young man decreasing down to a thirty-five hour week for the over fifty-fives. However, it is very doubtful if this would solve the problem because it is precisely those young workers who desire as much free time as possible, looking on work only as a means to an end. The purely sociological explanation of delinquency in terms of environment is only a partial answer. Only a small percentage of adolescent boys in any area join gangs. Most boys living in the same housing conditions manage to stay out of trouble and have no need of a violent gang. Psychological theories in terms of pathologically disturbed behaviour are also incomplete. Glueck's (1959) multidimensional interpretation, a 'dynamic interplay' of somatic, sociocultural and psychoanalytic factors, perhaps holds out some hope for understanding juvenile delinquency, suggesting its place within a coherent pattern of leisure life-style followed by a number of adolescents. Jephcott's (1967) research indicated that boys who later became leaders of gangs are known not only to the teachers at an early age but also to their fellow pupils who are apparently adept at spotting potential delinquents. Morse (1965) would appear to corroborate this view. It seemed generally agreed that, with a class of about thirty pupils, most teachers could identify the 'problem children'—the misfits, the anti-social, the troublemakers and potential troublemakers in and out of the school. 'If school dropouts, delinquent behaviour and frustration with the educational requirements of a society can be predicted long in advance, can we sit idly by and watch the prophecies come true? If remedial actions and therapy are less effective at later stages in the individual's development, can we satisfy a social conscience by indulging in such activities when it is far too late?' (Bloom, 1964).

Alcohol and sex. Why do adolescents drink? Alcohol (like certain other drugs) helps to reduce tension and anxiety; provides pleasant personal and social experiences; and can offer pseudo-resolutions of conflicts. Previously inhibited responses are loosened, and again curiosity, the influences of peers, a desire to appear grown up and the identification with adult models are influences on adolescent drinking patterns.

The average age of the alcoholic is falling—an increasing proportion have passed through the excessive and addictive stages to chronic alcoholism by the age of thirty years (Lane, 1974). The value of alcohol to the adolescent is of a symbolic (and not merely a functional) nature (i.e. usually drink is taken because of a desire to demonstrate toughness and maturity or as a means of attaining attractiveness and sociability often specifically with respect to the opposite sex). Many young people start to drink before they are eighteen; the age limit sanction is ineffective. They drink outside the home, away from adult concern and influence, so alcohol is associated with subterfuge and secrecy. Drinking among teenagers is on the increase. The majority of youngsters interviewed by Scarlett (1975) regularly used alcohol; of these fifty per cent were under age at the time. Most crucial of the complex reasons for alcohol consumption seemed to be adult models and the fact that both pubs and discotheques sell alcohol and are often the only places of entertainment in certain neighbourhoods.

The gap between physical and social maturity is widening in our society and greater strain is put on the adolescent in developing stable sexual patterns. Sex is a basic bodily function, but the adolescent's need for sexual identification is equally important. They have to test the strength of, and consolidate, their sexual identity in the light of possibly conflicting messages from behavioural models: peers, parents, teachers, pop stars, mass media. Pressure to conform to the norms of their subculture and identify with peers also influences adolescent sexual activity.

Further, there is now new openness about sex and sexual stimuli abroad for the adolescent—in music, books, films, television, and fashion. Changes in the social climate have produced greater equality between the sexes due to many factors, including the evidence and acceptance that women have sexual needs as great as men, and have a right to sexual satisfaction with chosen partners (Masters and Johnson, 1966); the increased efficiency and availability of contraception; fewer taboos about venereal disease and the fact that it is now more easily treatable; the availability of legal abortions; and changes in industry resulting in women's employment, and its consequences of relative familial and financial independence for women. But societal changes do not occur evenly nor concurrently so adolescents are caught in a 'double bind' of male-female differences and chastity-sexuality dilemmas, and they also receive conflicting social meanings and 'messages' from their adult role models. (Further, some models have not resolved their own double standards of behaviour.)

Cultural influences seem to be powerful determinants of basic differences between the sexes, and human sexual behaviour is strongly influenced by learning. What are these cultural influences? Firstly, the changing attitudes, behaviour patterns, and pluralistic values in society; secondly, social class background; and thirdly, subcultural beliefs, social patterns and life-styles. In this ever-changing situation research into sexual behaviour as a reflection of social and subcultural patterns may be one step behind; nevertheless general trends may be predicted. The Central Council for Health Education (1968), for instance, pointed out changes in attitude to pre-marital sex in a permissive direction, especially by girls. The majority of girls regarded sex as acceptable and permissible within a steady relationship, and it is possible to argue that this trend may continue for a time. As an indication of subcultural values, Kinsey et al (1948; 1953), Ford and Beach (1952) and Masters and Johnson (1966) have all reported certain class differences that could be related to values of gratification patterns and life-styles. Kinsey et al (1953) for example, pointed out that for adolescents from lower socio-economic groups pre-marital sex was many times more common, whereas in higher socio-economic groups heavy petting was indulged in, masturbation was more common and continued to a later age.

As a continuance of the theme that cultural influences effect sex differences Sharpe (1977) has pointed out the ways in which girls are influenced by the content of girls' comics and magazines. It is through this literature that expectations can be limited and personal confidence thwarted. As Sharpe (1977) wrote: 'They are very tuned in to the things that will bring social approval and quickly pick up cues from inside and outside the school'. She further suggested that there are pressures put on them from outside school to look 'sexy' and alluring and to view their goals in life as attracting a boy-friend, 'converting' him to husband, and being housekeeper and mother. Pressures are placed not only on females at an early age but on boys as well in our society. Sharpe (1977) suggested that 'Upper class boys at public schools are trained for leadership, business and the professions. At the other end of the scale, working class boys are schooled for a mass labour force which constrains many of the 'ideal' characteristics such as aggression and dominance, which in their work situation are potentially disruptive. *These are then transferred out on to leisure activities and particularly into their relationships with girls and women* [my italics]'. These dominant and aggressive tendencies are best revealed in quotations from researchers who have had first hand experience of working class gangs in America and Britain. As Yablonsky (1967) put it: 'The gang's relationships with girls were impersonal, brutal, aggressive and chauvinistic and they had a hatred for conventional boy-girl associations. The gang-bang is the ultimate virility symbol!'. Patrick (1970) suggested that the Glasgow gang member's attitude was one of arrogance and disdain:

' "Aw ra burds like gemme boays" ["All the girls like tough lads"] seemed to me central to the gang boy's view of relations with the opposite sex. In spite of a general contempt for girls, the gang was prepared to admit their occasional usefulness.'

This usefulness was specific, relatively impersonal and occurred in a group context rather as Yablonsky (1967) had outlined. Patrick (1970) continued:

> Tim, the leader of the Young Team, was at 15 already the father of an illegitimate child; all the boys in the gang, including the 14-year-olds, were sexually experienced. The general attitude to girls was epitomized in the gang 'aphorism', 'Shag 'em and sling 'em'. A general coarseness of behaviour and an absence of deep emotional commitment characterised most of the gang's dealings with girls, the majority of whom were again of school age.
>
> The girls who were constantly on the fringe of the gang were the type of adolescent who eventually ends up in a girls' Approved School on an order for care and protection. Three such girls had promiscuous relationships with the gang; they 'performed' numerous times on Friday and Saturday nights to deal with 'the big line-up' then followed them through the streets.
>
> Apart from these pathetic figures, the boys' more stable relationships with girls were still egocentric and based on physical dominance. Girls were camp followers rather than companions; they were 'at' the scene but not quite 'of' it. To Tim, girl friends, of which he had three in the four-month period I knew him well, were conquest objects which he used to prove and boost his masculinity. He hurled vile abuse at normal young couples in the district.

These patterns of sexual behaviour and attitudes of adolescent boys and girls can be related to general life-styles in that the middle classes believe in longer education and in receiving later economic independence thus necessitating greater containment of sexual urges and deferment of marriage. It should be noted, however, that these trends were discovered some years ago, and class differences in sexual behaviour in the 1970s may not manifest themselves in exactly the same way. Nevertheless, the point is that varying subcultural patterns *do* determine different life-styles and also reflect the 'respectable' conformity of certain groups, the 'experimental' versatility of others, and the 'meaningful' leisure patterns of working class groups as a resolution of wider social contradictions and conflicts.

Football and fanatics. Supporting professional football teams provides an obvious arena for aggression. Traces of 'oppositional' activity in behaviour are to be found in the expressive role of football supporter as against a passive acceptance of the role of spectator. Here, traditional working class concerns of neighbourhood, local identity, desire for participation and group solidarity may be linked with participation in acts of violence around soccer. Even here, however, the concern of soccer supporters in general is adaptive rather than directly oppositional—in that the violence linked with soccer represents an attempt to conserve traditional views of soccer from emasculation by an 'alien, and bourgeois, conception of soccer as business' (Taylor, 1971a, 1971b).

Taking the definition of a religion as a 'unified system of beliefs. and practices united into one single community', Coles (1974) said there is a 'football consciousness' which has become central to the life of supporters in which 'sacred' practices and rituals are observed. The separation from the world of work and leisure is facilitated not only by the wearing of special clothing, but also by exchanging feelings, sentiments and expectations—or several drinks. 'Each incident of the game is the basis of comment and reaction. Each expression of sentiment finds thousands more who wish to share it. In their every expression and agreement the feelings generated grow in intensity. Opinions which, in their expression, find the overwhelming agreement of vast crowds, become in their very utterance instant and powerful truths'.

The complete identification of spectator and player as the game proceeds is almost a religious experience. When the crowd sings 'We've won the cup', or 'We are the champions', this is not merely a victory for the team. 'Football is full of vicarious achievements and vicarious frustration' (Coles, 1974).

When achievement is frustrated and the 'unjustified' defeat has to be endured football comes nearest to a deeper religious expression. Most fans live in hope of better days, but for some the experience is hard to take. On the other hand success also can 'spill over' from 'religious' fervour and turn group gestures of victory into acts of euphoric aggression and violence.

Football is a good example of the particularly appealing powers of ritual. Crowds converse on the stadium, there is expression of emotion, patterns of support at the changes of fortune during the game, and finally the group disperses back to the city. Rituals serve to consolidate a group, but also delineate its separateness from other groups. Within the group it may also be possible to observe a hierarchy of supporter-roles which reinforce behaviour patterns. In part this may offer some insight into soccer hooliganism. On a simple level it is well known that each person in a crowd will demand a certain amount of personal space, and that as the crowd becomes larger and more tightly packed it often becomes uglier. These basic tensions, combined with patterns of support and aggressive life-styles all contribute to soccer violence and group vendettas.

Television and life styles. When the adolescent is free to do what he wants, he is likely to choose peer group oriented activities rather than those based on the home. Only television challenges the dominance of activities that include physical involvement in the group (such as visiting friends, hanging around in the street, or shopping with a friend or group of friends), or that are based on peer group values such as listening to records.

According to Murdock and Phelps (1973), eleven and twelve year olds watch an average of twenty hours of television a week. Their study revealed a considerable range in pupils' viewing habits; however about a third of fourteen and fifteen year old pupils, both boys and girls, claimed to watch more than four hours a night, which adds up to almost thirty hours of television a week. Forty per cent of pupils from lower working class homes claimed to watch four hours or more of television on an average weekday evening. The corresponding proportion for upper working class pupils was thirty five per cent and for middle class pupils twenty five per cent. It is possible that personality dictates choice even more than educational level or social class. Maccoby (1954) examined the extent of a child's interest in television as a symptom of the need for satisfaction through fantasy; for a programme to be interesting it must satisfy some personal need for the viewer. Maccoby suggested that fantasy activity as expressed in televiewing 'provides a child with experience which is free from real-life controls so that, in attempting to find solutions to a problem, he can try out various modes of action without risking the injury or punishment which might ensue if he experimented overtly'. This suggests that the television viewer is involved in a process of buffered learning similar to that hypothesised by Sutton-Smith (1964) which has equal educative potential for real-life situations.

Colemán (1961) suggested that the amount of use adolescents made of television could be shown on a graph as a U-shaped curve, with many high frequency viewers and many low frequency viewers, but with few subjects in the middle. Coleman postulated that this polarisation resulted from 'a kind of contagion effect, in which some viewing leads to more for those whose interest is captured, so that they "can't stop", while others never have their interest captured, but instead go on to other things'. Coleman's idea of polarisation lends support to Hendry and Patrick's (1977) suggestion that high and low frequency television viewers form sufficiently distinct groups for life-style profiles to be meaningful. The contrast between these two groups was more likely to be based on factors such as personality and academic attainment rather than on social factors, since no relationship was found between viewing frequency and social class. It may be that the clear social class differences in viewing found by Murdock and Phelps (1973) emerged because the adolescents in their sample attended three different kinds of school—grammar, comprehensive and secondary modern. Grammar school children who generally tend to be middle class, spent less time watching television because of the amount of homework they had to do. The schools attended by Hendry and Patrick's subjects were all comprehensive schools, where possibly less distinction was made between pupils than would be the case in the grammar school system. Thus middle class pupils might not necessarily have more homework in mid-adolescence and might be able to watch more television if they wished. (Since the comprehensive schools were situated in different areas: urban, suburban and new town areas, the sample was checked for differences among these areas but none were found.)

High and low frequency viewers were found to have different attitudes and values, which reinforces the apparent relation between types of viewers and personal rather than social class differences. High frequency viewers had a less favourable attitude to school, while girls who were high frequency viewers were more likely to think dancing and pop music were important. This fits in with the suggestion made by Murdock and Phelps (1973) that the worlds of school and the pop media are to some degree incompatible, to the extent that low frequency viewers were committed to the attitudes and values promoted by the school. This was related to the finding that high frequency viewers tended to do less well at school and tended to think it important to start work as soon as possible and to be earning money. Being at work would be associated with *not* being at school. Further, high frequency viewers were more likely to be bored in their leisure time than were low frequency viewers, which reflects the possibility that they rely to a great extent on 'available' external stimuli.

Perhaps it was to be expected both logically and empirically that high frequency viewing would be associated with a low level of sporting activity. High frequency viewers would have less time to indulge in sports; several studies found that television viewing increased in relation to decreased sporting activity (e.g. Coleman, 1961; Sillitoe, 1969; Emmett, 1971). As Hendry and Patrick's results on sport involvement indicated, habitual viewers spent their leisure time in more passive pursuits like reading or pottering about than did low frequency viewers. The differences between high and low frequency viewers suggested that the use adolescents make of television depends on personal characteristics (cf. Hendry & Thornton, 1976). The life styles of the two groups were quite different, with the high frequency viewers being more withdrawn and having few interests, while the low frequency viewers were more outgoing, popular and active, perhaps with less need to fill their time with television viewing.

Hendry and Patrick (1977) found a clear difference between sexes in the use they made of television. Boys and girls seem to differ in their use of television according to the sex roles ascribed to them by society; this claim is supported by the evidence about programme preferences. Boys were significantly more likely to watch factual programmes, in contrast to the films and plays preferred by girls. This difference may reflect the preoccupation of fifteen year old girls with the opposite sex and with romantic fiction found in popular girl's magazines such as 'Jackie' (Murdock & Phelps, 1973). On the other hand, it could be argued that female preference for plays and films reflect their superiority over adolescent males in terms of literacy and abstract thinking.

Klapper (1960) stated that differences in television viewing may be 'fundamental, probably permanent, and possibly related more to personality than social background'. Personality is obviously affected by pressures to conform to sex roles and these pressures may be important determinants of what adolescents watch on television, and the use they make of it in confirming their sex roles and personal identities. There is an obvious interaction between the medium and the viewer's motivations and values, and it is important to realise the 'active' role of the audience involved as they are with the subtleties of identification and gratification.

Mass media and life styles

The theory of uses and gratifications proposes that people make more or less use of television according to their own pre-existing needs; and that an audience's perception of what television has to offer depends not only on the content of the programmes but on the social and psychological characteristics of the audience. Perhaps this theory can also be used as a framework for looking at the mass media as a whole—television, pop culture, fashion and magazines—as manifestations of life-styles in leisure. Murdock and Phelps (1973) saw adherence to the pop culture as an expression of adolescent disengagement from school. Those children who cannot or do not follow the 'good pupil' role have two 'environmental cultures' to choose from as an expression of their disengagement from the culture of the school: the pop media and the street culture. Social class may determine which of these options the adolescent is likely to choose.

Murdock and Phelps (1973) identified three main clusters of pop styles, also showing that distinctions have to be made when discussing pop culture and adolescents. Using a small sample of fifteen year old pupils they found several distinctive features. While mainstream pop music was equally popular with middle class and working class adolescents; 'black music' (including reggae and soul) was predominantly followed by working class pupils; and 'heavy rock' was preferred by middle class teenagers. Murdock and Phelps saw results as indicating a tendency for middle class pupils, largely isolated from street culture values, to turn to certain types of pop music as a source of those values and roles undervalued by schools. But working class pupils were able to derive their alternative values from such street groups, and consequently pop culture was likely to be something which is part of the taken for granted background of group activities. Interest for these adolescents was not likely to extend beyond current hits. They found that fifty nine per cent of fourth formers interviewed would like various aspects of the pop culture—television, magazines, records—to be integrated into school courses; forty one per cent however said 'no'. Pupils who were unwilling for this study of contemporary 'common' culture to become part of school courses were more likely to be working class. In fact almost half of the working class pupils did not want such topics to become part of lessons, as compared to more than a quarter of middle class pupils. In this connection it is interesting to note the frequent changes in terminology. For example, as soon as 'punk rock' became accepted by the media as a descriptive term for that phenomenon, its street name changed to 'new wave'. These patterns can be related to life-styles, and it can be argued that the middle class pupils were more inclined to want the media in school in order to experience varying life-styles and patterns vicariously; working class pupils want to maintain a work-leisure division (and avoid 'establishment' terms) because they experience certain leisure styles and and use argot at first-hand.

The mass media may also have an influence on the way adolescents match their own self-esteem against social norms. In a study by Hendry and Gillies (1978) obese adolescents, especially girls, had a very low self-esteem in relation to their body, and Staffieri (1967) has pointed out that body build—with its associated expectations—becomes a framework for self-concept. Yet it can be argued that overweight girls approximate to 'the well proportioned feminine figure' mentioned by Clifford (1971) more closely than underweight adolescent girls. Hence despite self-esteem, their physique may allow them entry to the peer group; their drive for peer group acceptance may encourage behaviour which gains them group rewards. (It may not be without note that some adolescent boys' perceptions of popularity for girls was equated with promised or bestowed sexual favours.)

A different pattern emerged for 'underweight' adolescents. In leisure time, underweight adolescents were less involved with the opposite sex but more involved with television viewing than others. Hence in peer group relations, physique appears to have some influence on social interaction and choice of friends; the influence of a particular body type, namely being underweight and thin, causing some isolation and lack of contact with the opposite sex and greater involvement with television as Coleman (1961) postulated. There is some agreeement here with Cole's (1970) statement about the adjustment problems of adolescents possessing an 'inadequate' physique. This awareness may create uncertainty and withdrawal from the social (and perhaps particularly the sexual) scene, and produce a turning towards the vicarious pleasures of the mass media. It is clear that possession of particular body types has different meanings within adolescence in our society, meanings that are often transmitted by the media. In turn these differences create varying expectations, and behaviour patterns and life styles.

Concluding remarks. Leisure provision seems to be dominated by assumptions about certain activities being more valuable and worthwhile than others. Further, commercial leisure has produced institutionalised forms of individual or family leisure dominated by the cash nexus (i.e. the ability to pay). These movements towards conformity and institutionalisation have not been accomplished without some resistance. The significance of soccer hooliganism in this respect has been underlined (cf. Taylor, 1971). There is also evidence of adolescent life-styles which derive identification from subcultural attempts to resolve the contradictions of school and work situations in leisure styles. It has been suggested that these contradictions are mediations of social class differences (Murdock & Phelps, 1973): and if not strictly class based then certainly related to distinctive life-styles (Hendry & Thornton, 1976).

The class system is not necessarily dying and the provision of leisure facilities may, · if anything, be strengthening class differences. Local Authority provision of sports facilities has overtones of the old Public School 'moral code'—the idea that participation in sport leads to the development of such virtues as discipline and clear mindedness. The general feeling among many young people is that official youth clubs are too tame or over organised to appeal to them and that they are too much like school. Sports facilities of necessity require supervision and this fact increases their resemblance to school. These activities are rejected by adolescents who reject school, yet are accepted by those who accept school values (e.g. Jephcott, 1967; West, 1967; Hendry, 1975).

Hendry and Simpson (1977) found that one centre in a working class area with community facilities and sports facilities, housed two distinct groups of young people. One group were active sports members who found little to complain about in the facilities or staff. They travelled from a distance in order to use the sports facilities of the centre. The community users spent their time drinking coffee, 'chatting up the local talent', complaining about the facilities and staff and saying they were bored. They considered themselves trendy and the sports users as snobs and 'square'.

The sports group were those adolescents who accepted school values and had greater career aspirations. If not from middle class families they aspired to middle class values, and the activities they chose were in line with these values. The community group were local adolescents who rejected school and school values, who had limited aspirations for occupations and looked for more passive forms of recreation. The pattern of active or passive recreation activities has been suggested by several writers to be a function of social class. It certainly seems that in providing leisure facilities based on middle class assumptions, it is the middle class who make the fullest use of the facilities—so it is they who are further provided for at public expense. At the same time they make use of such low cost pursuits as hill walking and bird watching, often ignored by lower income groups (Burton, 1970). By providing certain types of facilities the middle class are further provided for while working class youths are not, thus a strengthening of social class differences into 'winners and losers' is promoted.

Another factor in determining types of leisure activity is the self concept of the adolescent. Murdock and Phelps (1973) claimed that the school is responsible (as a reflection of wider society) for casting types of self concept which are carried into leisure. The adolescent who drifts into deviant roles out of school is often the teenager who is stereotyped by those in the educational system as a failure because he does not conform to socially approved academic norms. Scarlett (1975) reported that there is more similarity between the same social class in different countries than between different classes in the same country. In examining what can be learnt from the rest of Europe he highlighted issues that Leigh (1971) outlined previously:

1 The need for existing facilities to be more readily available to people on terms realistically related to local conditions; and

2 The need for providers to explore the possibilities of non-institutional approaches.

Without such provision various 'deviant' patterns of subcultural life-styles may begin to emerge in leisure, reflecting particular value systems reinforced by adult models, and identification with peers. The result is conformity to the dominant ideology or the personal resolution of perceived contradictions within society. These subcultural leisure pursuits can include alcohol, sexual activity and general delinquent behaviour often within a gang. Obviously these activities result from a diversity of personal and socio-cultural factors but in all cases they result in clearly patterned life-styles. In this way, sports—in leisure as in school—can be seen as a reflection of conventional values set at counterpoint to a range of subcultural leisure pursuits which paradoxically also reflect adult models of behaviour.

APPENDIX

Appendix

Towards a typology

In an attempt to move towards a typology the author used the technique of cluster analysis. As Entwistle and Brennan (1971) have previously suggested any sample can be thought of as a distribution of points in hyperspace, analogous to stars in physical space. Just as matter is not equally distributed throughout the universe but condenses into stars held together in galactic formations of varying shapes, so points in psychological space may also produce regions of high or low destiny.

There are likely to be large tracts of relatively empty space populated by rare or unlikely kinds of pupils. Just as certain regions are empty, so others may be dense. Such high density regions may be regarded as continuous swarms of points (the galaxies of our cosmic analogy). The shape of the cluster is determined by the boundary conditions imposed by the computer programme on membership of a cluster. These limitations may be based on minimising the variance of the cluster, or on exploring variations in the density of points in hyperspace. Where distinct variations in density occur, the clusters are likely to be clearly defined whatever clustering procedure is adopted.

Cluster analysis was used to aid classification, and it was hoped to create a backcloth of evidence from which smaller scale 'illuminative' research investigations might be developed. The chief value of large scale research, in the author's mind, is to offer general evidence of possible trends or typologies which can then be studied at a more particularised level.

From the author's data on 3000 adolescents a separate cluster analysis for each group of variables designated as personal, social and educational factors was carried out for both boys and girls. In all this amounted to about 150 variables. Groupings for both boys and girls were sufficiently consistent and clear-cut to demand attention and consideration by a selected composite analysis (Figs. 5–7). For these composite clusterings two particular kinds of cluster analysis were employed:

1. Minimum spanning tree, which considers 'distances' among the 41 variables represented as points, and shows the pathways joining the (correlated) points. (It should be noted that there are *no* close loops, and *participation in school sports*

Fat

Body surface area

Neuroticism (r = -0.2)

Perceptual field independence

Height (r = 0.1)

Weight (r = 0.1)

Body esteem (r = +0.2)

Vertigo and aesthetic attitudes (r = 0.8)

Extraversion (r = +0.2)

Social
Cathartic
Health
Ascetic

Attitudes to sport (r = +0.3)

School sports participation

Speed and Fitness

Muscularity (r = +0.4)

Physical ability (r = +0.5)

NB A few original correlatives are given in brackets to provide some picture of the strength of associations.

Fig. 3. A diagrammatic representation of groupings of social factors associated with boys' and girls' participation in school sports

Family size and position in family

Siblings keen on sport

Encouragement from parents to engage in sports

Active leisure

Leisure sports involvement

School sports participation

Family considered to be important

Watching sport on T.V.

Sport seen as an important social value

Watch relatively little T.V.

Seldom bored in leisure

Social class

Important social attitudes and values, viz.:

Starting work as soon as possible

Earning money; treated as grown up

Clothes, appearance, hairstyle: job that's liked

Having a good time: dancing/discos, pop music

Having boy/girl friend: spare time spent with peers

Having friends to go around with

Academic
attainment
Advantages in R.O.S.L.A.
Favourable attitude to school

Member of school
(non-sporting) club

Attitudes
to school subjects

Social anxiety*

Position of
responsibility

Encouragement to
join community
sports and clubs

Desire to be better
at P.E. ø

Pupil's appearance*

Sport after
leaving school

Enthusiasm for
sport*

Pupil's attitude
to P.E. teacher ø

P.E. teacher's
attention ø

Physical
ability*

School
sports
participation

Competitiveness*

Enthusiasm ø
and
physical ability ø

Popular*
Friendly*

* denotes teacher's perceptions
ø denotes pupil's perceptions

the total length of the pathway is the minimum possible.) Thus it can 'say' something about clustering, if the measurement of the distance between clusters is taken to be the distance between the two nearest neighbours from two separate, i.e. different, clusters (Fig. 5). Further, we can break linkages (i.e. the first to be broken is the largest length, and so on) to create clusters. Those broken linkages lead us on to the second type:

2. Minimum variance cluster analysis. As with principal component analysis the distance between clusters is based on the sum of squares of the multidimensional planes (like multidimensional scaling, thus providing a 'cosmic' picture of galaxies and clusters (Fig. 6).

A number of points should be noted in relation to these diagrams or scatterplots. Firstly that the variables presented assume importance in relation to each other—in the diagram all is relative! Secondly, since the clusterings are shown two-dimensionally there is of necessity some pictorial distortion. Lastly, the 40 or so items presented were selected from the separate analyses because of their relative proximity to the 'sports participation' variable. The negative side of the picture, so to speak, is seen more clearly in the separate scatterplots (Figs. 2–4), where associations with non-participation are presented pictorially as diametrically opposed to school sports participation.

That said, a reasonably coherent pattern begins to emerge in the diagrams. For both boys and girls a grouping or clustering of physical and physiological components linked to physical education teachers' perceptions and pupils' own self estimates in relation to sports are seen to be most closely associated with school sports participation.

Within a second circle of constellated variables it can be noted that there is a relatively 'mixed' range of items linking 'home factors' such as parental encouragement, watching sport on television (secondary participation, Kenyon, 1968); 'social aspects' like leisure sports involvement, intentions to continue sport after leaving school; 'relational considerations' such as perceptions of and attitudes about physical education teachers; and 'personal factors', for instance, extraversion, attitudes to sport, body esteem and so on. Further, the pattern for boys and girls does show some variation at this level.

Social class, academic attainment, and favourable attitudes to school are shown to be closly linked—supporting incidentally a vast array of research findings—but a little distanced from school sports participation. This may raise important questions about the continuing influences of comprehensive education on pupils' extracurricular activities.

It is important at this stage to draw attention to a number of 'super' stars in our hyperspace. An examination of Figure 5 shows that certain variables are crucial centres linking the various elements of a psycho-social constellation. 'Enthusiasm for sports', 'physical ability' and 'involvement in school sport', all reveal several avenues converging on those variables. These may serve as aspects of concern for further investigation. Again the track between 'fitness' (distance run) and 'academic attainment' is fascinating because it raises questions about possible 'missing' variables—perseverance, motivation, achievement needs and such like. Further, a

involvement in physical activities (boys only)

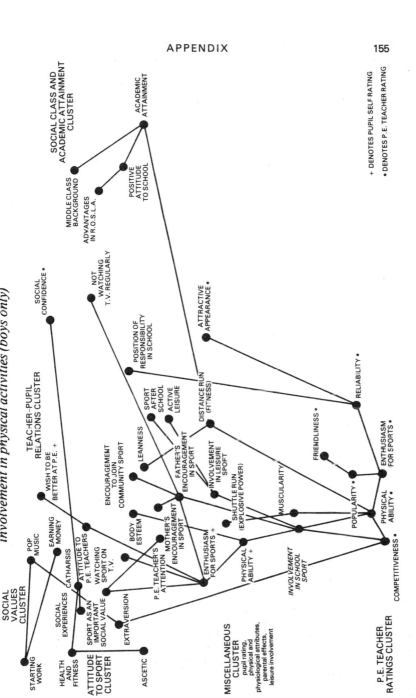

+ DENOTES PUPIL SELF RATING

● DENOTES P.E. TEACHER RATING

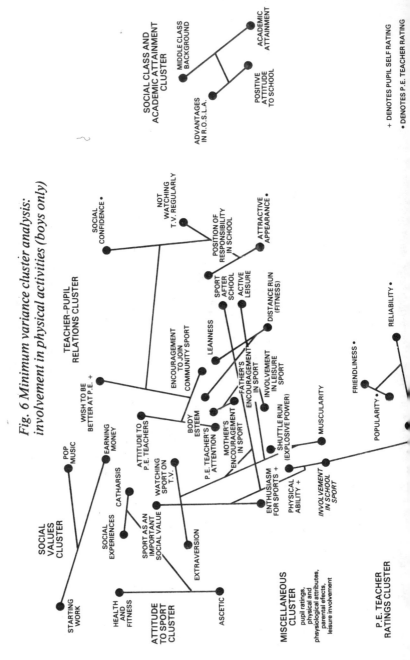

*Fig. 6 Minimum variance cluster analysis:
involvement in physical activities (boys only)*

SOCIAL CLASS AND ACADEMIC ATTAINMENT CLUSTER

MIDDLE CLASS BACKGROUND
ACADEMIC ATTAINMENT
ADVANTAGES IN R.O.S.L.A.
POSITIVE ATTITUDE TO SCHOOL

TEACHER–PUPIL RELATIONS CLUSTER

SOCIAL CONFIDENCE •
NOT WATCHING T.V. REGULARLY
POSITION OF RESPONSIBILITY IN SCHOOL
ATTRACTIVE APPEARANCE •
SPORT AFTER SCHOOL
ACTIVE LEISURE
DISTANCE RUN (FITNESS)
LEANNESS
ENCOURAGEMENT TO JOIN COMMUNITY SPORT
WISH TO BE BETTER AT P.E. +
INVOLVEMENT IN LEISURE SPORT
FATHER'S ENCOURAGEMENT IN SPORT
BODY ESTEEM
MOTHER'S ENCOURAGEMENT IN SPORT
P.E. TEACHER'S ATTENTION
SHUTTLE RUN (EXPLOSIVE POWER)
MUSCULARITY
ATTITUDE TO P.E. TEACHERS
WATCHING SPORT ON T.V.
ENTHUSIASM FOR SPORTS +
PHYSICAL ABILITY +
INVOLVEMENT IN SCHOOL SPORT

SOCIAL VALUES CLUSTER

POP MUSIC
EARNING MONEY
STARTING WORK
SOCIAL EXPERIENCES
CATHARSIS
SPORT AS AN IMPORTANT SOCIAL VALUE
EXTRAVERSION

ATTITUDE TO SPORT CLUSTER

HEALTH AND FITNESS
ASCETIC

FRIENDLINESS •
POPULARITY •
RELIABILITY •

MISCELLANEOUS CLUSTER
pupil ratings,
physical and
physiological attributes,
parental effects,
leisure involvement

P.E. TEACHER RATINGS CLUSTER

+ DENOTES PUPIL SELF RATING
• DENOTES P.E. TEACHER RATING

involvement in physical activities (girls only)

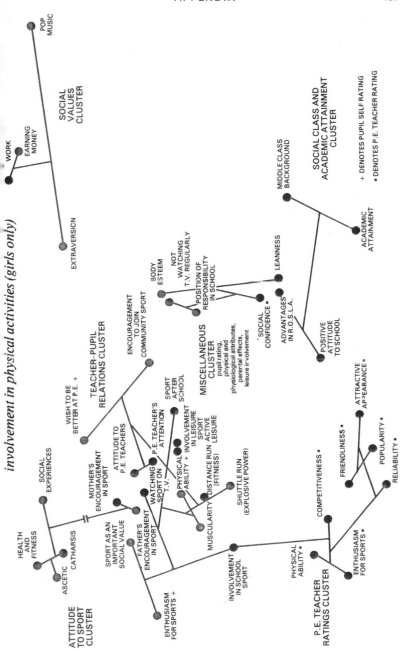

number of paths were associated with participation in physical activities, supporting McIntosh's (1963) and Kenyon's (1968) view that reasons for sports involvement are extremely complex.

Because of the nature of the author's investigation and the various ways in which data were collected it was impossible to classify certain items that may be important to sports involvement. For example, perceptions of sports participants by non-participants, and of non-participants by participants, were not ascertained simply because the researcher did not wish to make pupils consider possible differences between themselves and others within a school setting except in a very general way (but see Chapter 1), since the association between the author and the 15 schools continued for more than a year and there was some concern about possible shifts in 'self-esteem', and 'perceptions of others' during the actual investigation.

Adolescent groups seem reasonably accurate in estimating differences (as they perceive them) between sports participants and non-participants (see Hendry & Simpson, 1977) and such perceptions may be important in reinforcing attitudes, interests, and involvement in both school and leisure. Further, the author suggested (see Chapter 6) that sports participants at this particular age and level of involvement were provided with a wider network of social roles involving peers and adults—other sports participants, sports officials, friends, parents, and so on. Elsewhere it has been argued (Hendry, 1971; Tattersfield, 1971) that at a relatively high level of participation social roles are very much restricted to other athletes, coaches and sports administrators, with little time or opportunity to engage in a range of relationships with a variety of adolescent peers. If this is so it provides a restricted and narrow socilization process with limited access to 'appropriate' role models. It would be interesting to ascertain a 'cut off' point where the versatility of role possibilities proposed by the author in relation to sports participants ceases and the level of competitive sport precludes 'normal' adolescent socialization because of the commitment and dedication necessary for success. Nevertheless, given these limitations, a plausible general picture is evident which is reasonably consistent for both adolescent boys and girls.

If the offered general typology has any credence then a number of questons need to be asked about adolescents. What are the important links among physical ability, physique, and teachers' and pupils' perceptions in relation to pupils' personal characteristics and sports participation? What *practical* applicatons can be derived from the evidence that a number of links exist? Within comprehensive education there is still a strong association among social class, attitudes to school, attitudes to raising the school leaving age, and academic attainment: what are the reasons for this? Why are attitudes to work, to earning money, and to pop culture opposed to both scholastic attainment and sporting endeavour? Would studies of single schools reveal this same pattern? Would case studies and an 'illuminative' examination of teachers' and pupils' definitions and perspectives bring us closer to causal explanations?

It may be suggested that adolescent socialization into sport appears to 'fit in' with theories of the development of self by absorption of the perceptions and expectations of others. In this way self is seen as a social product. The adolescent's self identity develops in relation to the expectations and reactions of other people so that he reacts to himself as he perceives others reacting to him. Cluster analysis, in providing some move towards a typology, provides a broad outline and leads us to further important questions, most crucial of which perhaps is consideration of an analytical framework which encompasses the individual adolescent, and his self-esteem, in interaction with the various aspects of his culture (and subcultures) so that resultant socialization processes can be explored.

Obviously we must search for some kind of interpretative framework. More than this there is a need to progress from what is given—that is the behaviour, attitudes, involvements, perceptions of these adolescents, towards theory, to a set of predictions, explanations, interpretations and applications.

Rationale of the Scottish study

Most studies considering factors associated with pupil participation in physical activites have tended to concentrate on the relationship between participation and one category of variable (physiological, psychological, sociological, educational) but the author's investigation attempted to relate sports participation to a range of these categories, at times considering their interaction. While trying to take account of both the school system and individual pupils I have made no claim to present interaction fully from the position of the pupil or the researcher. Simply, I have tried to provide certain insights into pupil standpoints and values in relation to school, sports and leisure pursuits; and to compare these to teaching (and particularly the teaching of physical education) in schools.

Questions were formulated in an effort to study perceptions of both teachers and pupils (below the structural descriptive level), and in an attempt to establish insights into the possible links of the more general descriptive findings of the investigation. It was decided to select a sample of pupils prior to their school-leaving year and to follow them through their fourth year till they were sixteen years of age. A large number of these pupils were almost at the end of their school careers, and it could be reasonably assumed that at this stage their attitudes to and involvement in school, sports and leisure pursuits were well crystallized. The study considered secondary schools in one county, and from this fairly detailed analysis it may be possible to draw certain implications related to wider educational issues.

Stage of analysis—Level 1. The total pupil-sample was used in the descriptive analysis. That is, data were obtained for the majority of pupils on the following variables: height, weight, extraversion, neuroticism, embedded-figures test, six-sub-scales of attitude to physical activity, 600 yard and 5 x 20 yard fitness runs, social class academic attainment. In addition, teachers' assessments of pupils' physiques, personal characteristics and physical abilities were given for most pupils. Schools were classified into three broad socio-geographical categories: Suburban: 4; Urban: 6; New Town: 5; N = 15.

Level 2. From this list, twelve schools were selected to be considered for more detailed analysis. In addition to the data above, most pupils in the twelve schools completed a pupils' questionnaire to provide information about themselves, their attitude to school, physical activities and lesiure, thus providing deeper analysis at a descriptive level.

Level 3. Comparisons among five selected schools were carried out, and some attempt was made to study individual pupils within classes in two of the five schools. The intention of this approach was to examine 'the differing definitions' of teacher and pupil; and thus gain some insight into causal explanations of behaviour patterns of certain pupils. In addition, some general observations of the schools were carried out by the author.

The investigation was designed to take some account of teachers' and pupils' perceptions, particularly in relation to the descriptive variables, and to aspects of the physical education programme in schools. This approach enabled the researcher to avoid some of the participant-observer pitfalls outlined by Hargreaves (1967), though it is accepted, in turn, that it did prevent regular ongoing inquiry and interpretation at the face-to-face level with its situational specificity of meaning enjoyed by Hargreaves (1967), Keddie (1971), Beck (1972) and Nash (1973). On balance, however, the researcher felt that his approach allowed him some advantages of neutrality and of reasonable access to the general perceptions of both teachers and pupils, without too great an imposition of his own 'definition of the situation', and without the possible over-involvement of the social scientist with the social processes being studies.

Pilot studies. A number of limited studies were conducted prior to carrying out the investigation. Brief semi-structured interviews were conducted with university students, college of education students and 'early leavers' about present interests and involvement in physical activities, and about their views on the school's physical education programme. Involvement ranged from extreme enthusiasm to complete non-participation. Non-participants claimed to dislike institutionalized sport but were not against physical activities *per se.* Most queried why yoga, trampolining and other less structured activities were not included in physical recreation programmes, with a greater informality in approach.

Perhaps the greatest value to the researcher which emerged from these interviews was realisation of the wide range of opinions and views given, which led to the inclusion of a number of open-ended questions in the questionnaire to allow for the expression of personal opinion in an unstructured fashion.

In a general discussion about physical activities two groups of higher degree students including one group of experienced physical education teachers were asked to list the various personal, social and educational factors they personally considered to be most influential in determining an individual's participation in physical activities.

The items most frequently mentioned by students included sex, peers, physique, social class, parental influence, fitness, intelligence and personal attributes or personality.

Physical education teachers mentioned sex, school, physical education teachers, ability and/or skill, social factors, physique, personality, facilities, mass media, previous experience and local traditions or conditions.

This listing was most helpful in deciding which variables to include in the investigation.

Questionnaire construction. By using pilot samples of pupils of increasing numbers, opportunities were provided to determine both the appropriateness of questionnaire items, and the best procedures for administering them. For example, 750 pupils from three schools in central Scotland were selected to provide a full range of social class background and intellectual aptitude completed two questionnaires and one inventory. In addition, teachers at one school rated 200 pupils to pilot the teachers' assessment schedule.

Experience from such samples helped determine, for example, that a modified Likert version of Kenyon's (1968) Attitude Inventory should be used rather than the semantic differential approach and choice of vocabulary and degree of difficulty of statement-format was resolved.

A number of questions about teachers were posed in order to illumine teachers' personal constructs. For example what personal characteristics does the teacher use to describe a 'good' performer in physical activities? It might also be asked if teachers identify with, and have similar attitudes to, the more successful competitive pupils. Further, Hendry (1973) has suggested the possibility of a closed system in terms of ideologies and values, where the more successful pupils in turn become physical education teachers and perpetuate attitudes and practices. How, then, do teachers perceive the outcome of their secondary school physical education programmes, and what kind of teaching approach do they adopt—direct or individualised?

As for the pupils, to date no one has studied a wide range of personal, social and educational factors and considered which are the most significant in relation to physical activities involvement. It seems important in planning curricula to have such information; to consider if there are any activities which all pupils enjoy; to see if only certain individuals exhibiting recognisable behavioural characteristics actively involve themselves in sport.

Copeland (1972) has discussed the latent function of games in schools in relation to pupil status and attitudes, and it may be asked if active pupils have more favourable attitudes to school than non-participants. Furthermore, is sports activity a clear feature of identification with school-based values? What is the relationship between interest in time-tabled physical education and involvement in extracurricular school activities? What is the association between school based sports and leisure pursuits followed in the pupil's free time?

In terms of social aspects it is interesting to ask what influence home background has on participation. Is there a relationship between supportive families and sports involvement? Certainly social class has been shown to be related to sports involvement (Start, 1966), but is parental encouragement necessarily a class-based phenomenon in this instance?

In addition, the investigation made a general attempt to examine pupil and teacher perceptions. An important aspect of the investigation was the need to take into account the attitudes of individuals to each other. Questons we sought to answer included: how do pupils perceive their own abilities and enthusiasm for physical education; what were their views on physical education teachers and on the outcome of physical education programmes; how did they consider the attention given them by their physical education teacher; and what matching was there between the pupils' self-estimations and the perceptions of their teachers?

By studying a number of schools selected from the results of the descriptive analysis, and a number of individual pupils within these classes, it may be possible to move towards an examination of the ideologies behind the labelling processes of teachers, and the perceptions of pupils about teachers, physical activities and themselves. In this way the effects of general definitions of the situation can be considered, which may inform the ongoing face-to-face definitions of pupils and teachers which in turn affect enthusiasm, interest and involvement in physical activities.

REFERENCES

References

Albemarle Report (1960) *The youth service in England and Wales.* London: H.M.S.O.

Alexander Report (1975) *Adult education: The challenge of change.* London: H.M.S.O.

Atkin, R. (1976) White hopes or white elephants. *The Observer,* 7 March, 1976.

Argyle, M. (1972) *The social psychology of work.* London: Allen Lane, The Penguin Press.

Armstrong, H. E. & Armstrong, D. C. (1968) Relation of physical fitness to a dimension of body-image. *Percept. Motor Skills, 26,* 1173-4.

Bacon, W. (1975) Social caretaking and leisure provision. In S. Parker (Ed.) *Sport and leisure in contemporary society.* London: Central Polytechnic.

Ballantyne, W. (1974) A survey of the attitudes of some Glasgow school-children in Forms III and IV. Unpublished thesis. University of Glasgow.

Barker, R. G. & Gump, P. V. (1964) *Big school, small school.* California: Stanford University Press.

Barker-Lunn, J. C. (1970) *Streaming in the primary school.* Slough N.F.E.R.

Basini, A. (1975) Education for leisure: A sociological critique. In Haworth, J. T. & Smith, M.A. (Eds.) *Work and Leisure.* London: Lepus, 102-118.

Beck, J. (1972) Transition and continuity: a study of educational status passage. MA Thesis: University of London.

Bernstein, B. (1961) Social class and linguistic development: a theory of social learning. In A. H. Halsey, J. Flood & C. A. Anderson (Eds.) *Education, economy and society.* Glencoe: Free Press.

Bernstein, B. (1967) Open schools, open society? *New Society,* 14 September 351-353.

Bernstein, B., Elvin, H. L., & Peters, R. S. (1966) Ritual in education. *Phil. Transacts. of the Royal Soc., 251,* 429-436.

Berscheid, E. & Walster, E. (1972) Beauty and the beast. *Psychol. Today, 5,* 42-46.

Bloom, B. S. (1964) *Stability and change in human characteristics.* New York: Wiley, p. 231.

Blumler, J. G. & McQuail, D. (1968) *Television in politics: its uses and influences.* London: Faber and Faber.

Board of Education (1933) *Syllabus of physical training for schools.* London: H.M.S.O.

Bone, M. (1972) *The youth service and similar provision for young people.* London: H.M.S.O.

Brooke Taylor, G. (1970) Quality in recreation. In T. L. Burton (Ed.) Recreation, research and planning, *Urban and Regional Studies* 1.

Brookover, W. B., Erickson, E. L. & Jones, L. M. (1967) Self-concept of ability and school achievement III. Educ. Publishing Services, College of Education, University of Michigan.

Brookover, W. B., Le Pere, J. M., Hamachek, D. E., Shailer, T. & Erickson, E. L. (1965) Self-concept of ability and school achievement II. Educational Research Series, 31, Bureau of Educ. Res. Services, College of Education, University of Michigan.

Burton, T. L. (1970) Current trends in recreation demands. In T. L. Burton (Ed.) *Recreation research and planning.* London: Allen & Unwin.

Byrne, D., London, O. & Reeves, K. (1968) The effects of physical attractiveness, sex, and attitude similarity on interpersonal attraction. *J. Person., 36,* 259–271.

Carroll, R. (1976) Evaluating lessons. *Brit J. Phys. Educ., 7,* 6, 202–203.

Carter, M. (1972) The world of work and the R.S.L.A. pupil. *Education in the North, 9,* 61–64.

Central Council for Health Education (1966) *Sexual behaviour of young people.* London: H.M.S.O.

Clifford, E. (1971) Body satisfaction in adolescence. *Percept. Motor Skills, 33,* 119–125.

Clifford, M. M. & Walster, E. (1973) The effect of physical attractiveness on teacher expectations. *Sociol. Educ., 46,* 248–258.

Cohen, A. K. (1950) *Delinquent boys.* London: Routledge & Kegan Paul.

Cole, L. & Hall, I.N. (1970) *Psychology of adolescence.* New York: Holt, Rinehart & Winston.

Coleman, J. S. (1961) *The adolescent society.* Glencoe: Free Press.

Coles, R. (1974) *A sociological year book of religion.* London: S.C.M. Press.

Collins, M. & Rees, B. (1975) Sport in an urban context. In S. Parker (Ed.) *Sport and leisure in contemporary society.* London: Central Polytechnic.

Copeland, I. C. (1972) The function of sport in secondary education. *Educ. Rev., 25,* 1, 34–45.

Council of Europe (1976) Geneva: U.N.E.S.C.O.

Crawford, S. (1976) Violence in rugby. *Br. J. Phys. Ed., 7,* 6.

Crunden, C. (1970) Sport and social class: a study of 13 and 15 year old children. *Bull. Phys. Educ., 8,* 37.

Cumming, G. R. (1971) Correlation of physical performance with laboratory measures of fitness. In R. J. Shephard, (Ed.) *Frontiers of fitness.* Springfield, Illinois: Thomas.

Daniel, S. & McGuire, P. (1972) *The paint house: words from an east-end gang.* Harmondsworth: Penguin.

Darling, R. C. (1947) The significance of physical fitness. *Arch. Phys. Med., 28,* 140.

Davidson, H. H. & Lang, G. (1966) Children's perceptions of their teachers' feelings towards them related to self-perception, school achievement and behaviour. *J. Exper. Educ., 29,* 2, 107.

Davies, R. D. S. (1970) Youth service as a part of further education. In I. Bulman, M. Craft & F. Milson (Eds.) *Youth service and interprofessional studies.* London: Pergamon Press.

Dion, K. (1972) Physical attractiveness and evaluation of children's transgressions. *Jour. Pers. Soc. Psychol., 24,* 207–213.

Douglas, J. D. (1967) *The social meaning of suicide.* New Jersey: Princeton University Press.

Douglas, J. W. B. (1964) *The home and the school.* London: MacGibbon & Kee.

Douglas, J. W. B., Ross, J. M. & Simpson, H. R. (1968) *All our future.* London: Peter Davies.

Douglas, M. (1966) *Purity and danger: an analysis of concepts of pollution and taboo.* London: Routledge & Kegan Paul.

Douvan, E. & Adelson, J. (1966) *The adolescent experience.* New York: Wiley.

Douvan, E. & Kaye, C. (1967) *Adolescent girls.* Ann Arbor: University of Michigan.

Duffy, A. B. (1972) Expression of curiosity, interest and retention. Unpublished MA Thesis, University of Southampton.

Durnin, J. V. G. A. (1967) Activity patterns in the community. In International symposium on physical activity and cardiovascular health. *Canad. Med. Assoc. J., 96,* 882–885.

Dwyer, J. & Mayer, J. (1967) Variations in physical appearance during adolescence. (Part I: Boys) *Postgrad. Med., 41,* 99–107.

Eggleston, J. (1976) *Adolescence and Community.* London: Arnold.

Eggleston, J. (1975) Conflicting curriculum decisions. *Educ. Studies, 1,* 1, 3–8.

Eggleston, J. (1965) Secondary schools and Oxbridge blues. *Brit. J. Sociol., 16,* 3, 232–242.

Elder, G. H. (1968) Adolescent socialisation and development. *Handbook of personality theory and research.* Chicago: University Press.

Emmett, I. (1970) Sociological research in recreation. In T. L. Burton (Ed.) *Recreation research and planning.* London: Allen & Unwin.

Emmett, I. (1971) *Youth and leisure in an urban sprawl.* Manchester: University Press.

Entwistle, N. J. & Brennan, T. (1971) Types of successful students. *Brit. J. Educ. Psychol., 41,* 3, 268–276.

Erikson, E. H. (1968) *Identity, youth and crisis.* New York: Norton.

Esterton, A. (1972) *The leaves of spring: schizophrenia, family and sacrifice.* Harmondsworth: Penguin.

Eysenck, H. J. (1964) *Crime and personality.* London: Routledge & Kegan Paul.

Eysenck, H. J. (1967) *The biological basis of personality.* Springfield, Illinois: Thomas.

Eysenck, H. J. & Eysenck, S. B. G. (1964) *Manual of the Eysenck personality inventory.* London: University Press.

Fast, J. (1970) *Body language.* New York: Evans.

Fitzpatrick, P. (1976) *The Guardian,* Friday, 17 December.

Fleishman, E. A. (1964) *Examiner's manual for the basic fitness tests.* Englewood Cliffs, New Jersey: Prentice-Hall.

Fleishman, E. A. (1967) Individual differences and motor learning. In Gagne, R. M. (Ed.) *Learning and individual differences.* Ohio: Merrill.

Fogelman, K. (1976) *Britain's sixteen year olds,* London. Nat. Child. Bureau.

Ford, C. S. & Beach, F. A. (1952) *Patterns of sexual behaviour.* London: Eyre & Spottiswoode.

Foster, G. G., Ysseldyke, J. E. & Reese, J. H. (1975) I wouldn't have seen it if I hadn't believed it. *Except. Child.,* April, 469–473.

Fowler. P. (1972) Skins rule, In C. Gillet (Ed.) *Rock file.* London: Pictorial Publications.

Fraser, E. (1959) *Home environment and the school.* London: University Press.

Giddens, A. (1964) Notes on the concepts of play and leisure. *Sociol. Rev., 12,* 73–89.

Glasser, R. (1970) *Leisure, penalty or prize.* London: Macmillan.

Glueck, S. (1959) Theory and fact in criminology. In *The problem of delinquency,* pp. 241–252.

Goffman, E. (1959) *Presentation of self in everyday life.* New York: Doubleday, Anchor Books.

Goldethorpe, D. & Lockwood, J. (1968) *The affluent worker in the class structure.* Cambridge: University Press.

Gordon, W. T. (1957) *The social system of the high school.* Glencoe: The Free Press.

Grace, G. R. (1974) Vulnerability and conflict in the teaching role. In J. Egglestone (Ed.) *Contemporary research in the sociology of education.* London: Methuen.

Hallworth, H. J. (1961) Teachers' personality ratings of high school pupils. *Jour. Educ. Psychol., 52,* 297–302.

Hallworth, H. J. (1962) A teacher's perceptions of his pupils. *Educ. Rev., 14,* 124–133.

Hallworth, H. J., Davis, H. & Camston, C. (1965) Some adolescents' perceptions of adolescent personality. *J. Soc. Psychol., 4,* 81–89.

Hammar, S. L. (1965) The obese adolescent. *Jour. School Health, 35,* 246–249.

Hardman, K. (1962) An investigation into the possible relationships between athletic ability and certain personality traits in third year secondary modern schoolboys. Diploma dissertation: University of Manchester.

Hardman, K. (1973) A dual approach to the study of personality and performance in sport. In Whiting, H. T. A., Hardman, K., Hendry, L. B. & Jones, M. G. *Personality and performance in physical education and sport*. London: Kimpton.

Hargreaves, D. H. (1967) *Social relations in a secondary school*. London: Routledge & Kegan Paul.

Hargreaves, D. H. (1972) *Interpersonal relations and education*. London: Routledge & Kegan Paul.

Hargreaves, D. H., Hestor, S. K. & Mellor, F. J. (1975) *Deviance in classrooms*. London: Routledge & Kegan Paul.

Harper, D., Munro, J. & Himmelweit, H. T. (1970) Social and personality factors associated with children's tastes in television viewing. In J. Tunstall (Ed.) *Media Sociol.*, London: Constable, pp. 363–71.

Heinila, K. (1964) The preferences of physical activities. In Jokl, E. & *Simm, E. (Eds.) International research in sport and physical education*. Springfield, Illinois: Thomas.

Helanko, R. (1957) Sports and socialization. *Acta Sociologica*, 2.

Hendry, L. B. (1970) Some notions on personality and sporting ability: certain comparisons with scholastic achievement. *Quest, 13*, 63–73.

Hendry, L. B. (1971) Don't put your daughter in the water, Mrs Worthington? (A sociological examination of the subculture of competitive swimming). *Br. J. Phys. Educ.*, *2*, 3, 17–29.

Hendry, L. B. (1973) The physical educationalist stereotype. In Whiting, H. T. A., Hardman, K., Hendry, L. B. & Jones, M. G. *Personality and performance in physical education and sport*, 123–148. London: Kimpton.

Hendry, L. B. (1974a) Involvement in physical activities: speculation and findings. In Brooke, J. D. (Ed.) *Proceedings of the British Sports Psychology Society Conference*, University of Salford, September, 57–78.

Hendry, L. B. (1974b) Involvement in physical activities: structure and infra-structure. *Proceedings of the 10th European Conference on Psychosomatic Research*. University of Edinburgh, September.

Hendry, L. B. (1975) School, sport, leisure: a study of personal social and educational factors. Report to the Scottish Education Department, Edinburgh.

Hendry, L. B. (1975a) The role of the physical education teacher. *Educ. Res. 17*, 2, 115–121.

Hendry, L. B. (1975b) Survival in a marginal role: the professional identity of the physical education teacher. *Br. J. Sociol., 26*, 4, 465–76.

Hendry, L. B. (1976) Early school leavers, sport and leisure. *Scott. Educ. Studies 8*, 1, 48–51.

Hendry, L. B. & Aggleton, P. (1977) Teaching styles in physical education. Unpublished memorandum. University of Aberdeen.

Hendry, L. B. & Douglass, L. (1975) University students: attainment and sport. *Br. J. Educ. Psychol., 45*, 299-306.

Hendry, L. B. & Gillies, P. (1978) Body type, body esteem, school and leisure: a study of overweight, average and underweight adolescents. *J. Youth and Adol., 7*, 20.

Hendry, L. B. & Lee, A. (1976a) Sports involvement of student teachers. *Br. J. Phys. Educ., 7*, 1, 25-26.

Hendry, L. B. & McIntyre, R. (1976b) Professional courses in physical education: student selection and characteristics. *Scott. J. Phys. Educ., 4*, 1, 12-16.

Hendry, L. B. & Patrick, H. (1977) Adolescents and television, *Jour. of Youth and Adol. 7*, 3, 2, 321-334.

Hendry, L. B. & Simpson, D.O. (1977) One centre; two subcultures. *Scott. Educ. Studies, 9*, 2, 112-121.

Hendry, L. B. & Thornton, D. (1976) Games theory, television and leisure in adolescent study. *Br. J. Soc. Psychol., 15*, 369-76.

Herbert, J. F. (1965) The influence of personality and games ability upon physical skill performed under stress. Unpublished diploma dissertation. University of Manchester.

Herbert, J. F. & Steel, W. L. (1968) The influence of personality and games ability upon a throwing skill performed under stress. *Res. Phys. Educ., 1*, 3, 12-17.

Himmelweit, H. T., Oppenheim, A. N. & Vince, P. (1958). *Television and the child.* Oxford: University Press.

Horrocks, J. E. (1951) *The psychology of adolescence.* New York: Houghton Mifflin.

Hoyle, E. (1969) *The role of the teacher.* London: Routledge & Kegan Paul.

Hoyle, E. (1971) In Hopper, R. (Ed.) *The curriculum: context, design and development.* Edinburgh: Oliver & Boyd, Part III, Ch. 1.

Illich, I. (1971) *Deschooling society.* London: Harper & Row.

Jackson, P. W. (1968) *Life in classrooms.* London: Holt, Rinehart & Winston.

Jackson, P. W. & Getzels, J. W. (1959) Psychological health and classroom functioning: A study of dissatisfaction with school among adolescents. *J. Educ. Psychol., 50.*

Jackson, P. W. & Lahaderne, H. M. (1967) Scholastic success and attitude towards school in a population of sixth graders. *J. Educ. Psychol., 58*, 1, 15-18.

Jephcott, P. (1967). *Time of one's own.* Edinburgh: Oliver & Boyd.

Kagan, J. (1967) On the need for relativism. In Hudson, L., *The ecology of human intelligence.* Harmondsworth: Penguin.

Kagan, J. & Moss, H. (1962) *Birth to maturity.* New York: Wiley.

Kalton, G. (1966) *The public schools.* London: Longmans.

Kane, J. E. (1962) Physique and physical abilities of fourteen year old boys in relation to personal and social adjustment. MEd thesis. University of Manchester.

Kane, J. E. (1964) Psychological correlates of physique and physical abilities. In Jokl, E. & Simon, B. (eds.) *International research in sport and physical education.* Springfield, Illinois: Thomas.

Kane, J. E. (1969) Body type and personality. *Res. Phys. Educ., 1,* 4.

Kane, J. E. (1972) Personality, body concept and performance. In Kane, J. E. (Ed.) *Psychological aspects of physical education and sport.* London: Routledge & Kegan Paul.

Kane, J. E. (1974). *Physical education in secondary schools.* Schools' Council Research Studies. Basingstoke & London: Macmillan.

Keddie, N. (1971) Classroom knowledge. In M. D. F. Young (Ed.) *Knowledge and control.* London: Collier MacMillan.

Kelly, G. A. (1955) *The psychology of personal constructs.* New York: Norton.

Kenyon, G. S. (1968a) A conceptual model for characterising physical activity. *Res. Quart., 39,* 96–105.

Kenyon, G. S. (1968b) Six scales for assessing attitude toward physical activity. *Res. Quart., 39,* 566–574.

Kenyon, G. S. (1968c) Values held for physical activity by selected urban secondary school students in Canada, Australia, England and the United States. United States Office of Education, Contract S–376, University of Wisconsin.

King, R. (1973) *School organisation and pupil involvement: a study of secondary schools.* London: Routledge & Kegan Paul.

Kinsey, A. C., Pomeroy, W. B. & Martin, C. E. (1948) *Sexual behaviour in the human male.* Philadelphia: Saunders.

Kinsey, A. C., Pomeroy, W. B., Martin, C. E. & Gebhard, P. H. (1953) *Sexual behaviour in the human female.* Philadelphia: Saunders.

Klapper, J. T. (1960) *The effects of mass communication.* Glencoe: The Free Press.

Klein, J. (1965) *Samples from English cultures.* London: Routledge & Kegan Paul.

Lacey, C. (1966) Some sociological concomitants of academic streaming. *Br. J. Sociol., 17,* 245–262.

Lacey, C. (1970) *Hightown Grammar: the school as a social system.* Manchester University Press.

Lambert, R., Bullock, R. & Millham, S. (1973) The informal system. In Brown, R. (ed.) *Knowledge, education and cultural change.* London: Tavistock.

Lane, D. A. (1974) Drugs Education. In *Educational Research,* Vol. 16

Layman, E. McC. (1972) The contribution of play and sports to emotional health. In J. E. Kane, (Ed.) *Psychological aspects of physical education and sport.* London: Routledge & Kegan Paul.

Lee, S. F. (1968) The role of the male teacher of physical education as perceived by men students at two colleges. Unpublished diploma dissertation. University of Manchester.

Leigh, J. (1971) *Young people and leisure.* London: Routledge & Kegan Paul.

Lerner, R.M. (1969) The development of stereotyped expectancies of body-build relations. *Child Dev., 50,* 137–141.

Lerner, R. M. (1969a) Some female stereotypes of male body-build behaviour relations. *Percept. Mot. Skills, 28,* 363–366.

Lindsay, C. (1969) *School and community*. London: Pergamon.

Little, A. & Westergaard, J. (1964) The trend of class differentials in England and Wales. *Br. J. Sociol., 15*, 3, 311–314.

Lotwick, W. R. (1965) Quoted in Smithers et al. (q.v.)

McClelland, D. C. (1961) *The achieving society*. Princeton: Van Nostrand.

Maccoby, E. E. (1954) Why do children watch television? *Public Opinion Quart., 18*, 239–244.

McKay, H. D. (1959) The neighbourhood and child conduct. In Glueck, S. (Ed.) *The problem of delinquency*. Cambridge, Mass: The Riverside Press.

McIntosh, P. C. (1963) *Sport in society*. London: Watts.

McIntosh, P. C. (1966) Mental ability and success in school sport. *Res. in Phys. Educ., 1*, 1, 20–27.

Manners, R. C. & Velden, L. V. (1974) The relationship between professionalization of attitude toward play in pre-adolescent boys and participation in organized sport. In G. H. Sage (Ed.) *Sport and American society*. Reading, Mass: Addison-Wesley.

Masters, W. H. & Johnson, V. E. (1966) *Human sexual response*. London: Churchill.

Matza, D. (1964) *Delinquency and drift*. New York: Wiley.

Matza, D. & Sykes, G. (1961) Juvenile delinquency and subterranean values. *American Sociological Review, 26*, 712–19.

Mays, J. B. (1965) *Education and the urban child*. Liverpool: University Press.

Mead, G. H. (1934) *Mind, self and society*. Chicago: University Press.

Merton, R. K. (1949) *Social theory and social structure*. Glencoe: The Free Press.

Meyersohn, R. (1968) Television and the rest of leisure. *Public Opin. Quart., 32*, 102–112.

Midwinter, E. (1972) *Projections: an educational priority area at work*. London: Ward Lock.

Miller, D. (1966) Leisure and the adolescent. *New Society*, 9 June, 8–10.

Miller, J. O. (1967) Longitudinal analysis of the relationship of self-differentiation and social interaction and selected physical variables in boys twelve to seventeen years of age. PhD thesis. University of Oregon.

Milson, F. (1972) *Youth in a changing society*. London: Routledge & Kegan Paul.

Mitchell, S, & Shepherd, M. (1967) The child who dislikes going to school. *Brit. J. Psychol., 37*, 32–40.

Molyneux, D. (1975) Planning and provision for recreation. In S. Parker (Ed.) *Leisure and public policy*. L.S.A.

Monks, T. G. (1968) *Comprehensive education in England and Wales*. Slough Nat. Found. Educ. Res.

Morse, M. (1965) *The unattached*. Harmondsworth: Pelican Books, p.147.

Morrison, A. & Hallworth, H. J. (1966) The perception of peer personality by adolescent girls. *Br. J. Educ. Psychol., 36*, 241–247.

Morton-Williams, R. & Finch, S. (1968) *Enquiry I: young school leavers.* London: H.M.S.O.

Munrow, A. D. (1971) Identity in modern society—the contribution of sport and physical education. *Educ. & Culture, 15, 21-26.*

Munrow, A. D. (1972) *Physical education: a discussion of principles.* London: Bell.

Murdock, G. & Phelps, G. (1973) *Mass media and the secondary school.* London: Macmillan.

Musgrove, F. (1964) *Youth and the social order.* London: Routledge & Kegan Paul.

Musgrove, F. & Taylor, P. H. (1969) *Society and the teacher's role.* London: Routledge & Kegan Paul.

Mussen, P. (1973) *The psychological development of the child.* Englewood Cliffs, N. J.: Prentice-Hall.

Nash, R. (1973) *Classrooms observed.* London: Routledge & Kegan Paul.

Nash, R. (1976) *Teacher Expectations and Pupil Learning.* London: Routledge & Kegan Paul.

Neulinger, J. & Breit, M. (1969) Attitude dimensions of leisure. *J. Leisure Res., 1, 255-261.*

Neulinger, J. & Breit, M. (1971) Attitude dimensions of leisure: a replication. *J. Leisure Res., 3, 108-115.*

Newsom Report (1963) *Half our future.* London: H.M.S.O.

Nichols, A. K. (1971) The field dependence—field independence personality dimensions and games attainment in schoolboys. *Bull. of Phys. Educ., 8, 6, 10-16.*

Nichols, A. K. (1974) Attitudes to physical activity and some associated variables amongst secondary school children. In J. D. Brooke, (Ed.) *Proceedings of the British Sports Psychology Society Conference.* University of Salford, September, 92-107.

Ogilvie, B. (1968) Psychological consistencies within the personality of high level competitors. *J. Amer. Med. Assoc.,* Special Report, 205.

Orlick, T. D. (1972) A socio-psychological analysis of early sports participation. PhD Thesis: University of Alberta.

Orwell, G. (1934) *England your England and other essays.* London: Methuen.

Parnell, R. W. (1954) Physique and performance. Honours class at Oxford. *Br. Med. J., 2, 49-66.*

Parnell, R. W. (1958) *Behaviour and physique.* London: Arnold.

Parry, N. & Johnson, D. (1975) Sociology and leisure. In S. Parker (Ed.) *Sport and leisure in contemporary society.* London: Central Polytechnic.

Parsons, J. M. (1973) Prediction of athletic performance through physique classification. *Br. J. Phys. Educ., 4, 4, 11-14.*

Patrick, J. (1970) *A Glasgow gang observed.* London: Methuen.

Pedley, R. (1956) *Comprehensive education.* London: Gollancz.

Rapoport, R. & Rapoport, R. N. (1974) Four themes in the sociology of leisure. *Br. J. Sociology, 25,* 215–229.

Read, D. A. (1969) The influence of competitive and non-competitive programmes of physical education on body image and self concept. *Annual Proceedings* of N.C.P.E.A.M., A.A.H.P.E.R., Washington.

Reynolds, R. M. (1965) Responses on the Davidson Adjective Check List as related to maturity, physical and mental characteristics of thirteen-year old boys. PhD dissertation, University of Oregon.

Reid, M. (1972) Comprehensive integration outside the classroom. *Educ. Res., 14,* 2, 128–134.

Richer, R. L. (1968) Schooling and the self-concept. *New Era, 49,* 7.

Rist, R. C. (1970) Student social class and teacher expectations: the self-fulfilling prophecy in ghetto education. *Harvard Educ. Rev., 40,* 3, 411–451.

Robinson, W. P. (1975) Boredom at school. *Br. J. Educ. Psychol., 45,* 141–152.

Rodgers, H. B. (1974) *Planning for leisure.* Coventry: University of Warwick.

Rosenberg, M. (1965) *Society and the adolescent self-image.* New Jersey: Princeton University Press.

Rosenthal, R. & Fode, R. L. (1963) The effect of experimenter bias on the performance of albino rats. *Behav. Sci., 8,* 183–189.

Rosenthal, R. & Jacobson, L. (1968) *Pygmalion in the classroom.* New York: Holt, Rinehart & Winston.

Ross, J. M. (1973) The physical education departments of twelve comprehensive schools. *Br. J. Phys. Educ., 4,* 2, 9–12.

Saunders, E. D. & Witherington, K. S. (1970) Extra-curricular physical activities in the secondary school. *Br. J. Phys. Educ., 1,* 1, 10–14.

Sauer, L. W. (1966) Your adolescent's health. *P.T.A. Mag., 60,* 31–32.

Scarlett, C. L. (1975) *Euroscot: the new European generation.* The Scottish Standing Conference of Voluntary Youth Organisations, Edinburgh.

Schofield, M. (1965) *Sexual behaviour of young people.* London: Longman.

Schools' Council (1968) Objectives of physical education. *Dialogue, 1, 15.*

Scottish Education Department (1972) *Curriculum Paper 12: Physical education in secondary schools.* Edinburgh: H.M.S.O.

Sharpe, S. (1977) *Just like a girl, How girls learn to be women.* Harmondsworth: Pelican.

Sheldon, W. H. & Stevens, S. S. (1942) *The varieties of temperament.* New York: Harper.

Shipman, M. D. (1968) *Sociology of the school.* London: Longman.

Sigall, H., Page, R. & Brown, A. C. (1971) Effort expenditure as a function of evaluation and evaluator attractiveness. *Rep. Res. Soc. Psychol., 2,* 19–25.

Sillitoe, K. K. (1969) *Planning for leisure.* London: H.M.S.O.

Simpson, J. (1973) Education for leisure. In Smith, M., Parker, S., & Smith, C. (Eds.) *Leisure and society in Britain.* London: Allen Lane.

Smith, C. S. (1973) Adolescence. In M. A. Smith, S. Parker & C. S. Smith (Eds.) *Leisure and society in Britain*. London: Allen Lane.

Smith, H. M. & Clifton, M. A. (1962) Sex differences in expressed self-concepts concerning the performance of selected motor skills. *Percept. Motor Skills, 14,* 71–73.

Smithers, A. Ávis, G. & Lobley, D. (1974) Conceptions of school among pupils affected by the raising of the leaving age. *Educ Res., 16,* 210–17.

Spady, W. (1970) Lament for lettermen: effects of peer status and extra-curricular activities in goals and achievement. *Amer. J. Sociol., 74,* 630–720.

Spencer, C. P. (1972) Selective secondary education, social class and development of academic sub-cultures. *Br. J. Educ. Psychol., 42,* 1–13.

Sports Council (1968) *Planning for sport.* Central Council of Physical Recreation, London.

Sports Council (1971) *Indoor sports centres.* London: H.M.S.O.

Staffieri, J. F. (1967) A study of social stereotype of body image in children. *J. Pers. Soc. Psychol., 7,* 1, 101–104.

Stanaway, R. G. & Hullin, R. P. (1973) The relationship of exercise response to personality. *Psychol Med., 3,* 343–349.

Standing Consultative Council on Youth and Community Service (1968) *Community of interests.* Edinburgh: H.M.S.O.

Start, K. B. (1961) The relationship between games performance of a grammar school boy and his intelligence and streaming. *Br. J. Educ. Psychol., 31,* 2, 208–211.

Start, K. B. (1963) Group interaction and examination results. *Phys. Educ., 55,* 166.

Start, K. B. (1966) Substitution of games performance for academic achievement as a means of achieving status among secondary school children. *Brit. J. Sociol., 17,* 3, 300–305.

Stenhouse, L. (1975) *An introduction to curriculum, research and development.* London: H. E. B.

Stunkard, A. J. & Mendelson, M. (1967) Obesity and the body image. Characteristics of disturbances in the body image of some obese persons. *Amer. Jour. Psychist., 123,* 1296–1300.

Sugarman, A. A. & Haronian, F. (1964) Body-type and sophistication of body concept. *J. Person., 32,* 380–394.

Sugarman, B. (1967) Involvement in youth culture, academic achievement and conformity in school. *Br. J. Sociol., 18,* 157–164.

Sugarman, B. (1968) The social system of the school. British Sociological Association Annual Conference.

Sutton-Smith, B. & Roberts, J. M. (1964) Rubrics of competitive behaviour. *J. Genet. Psychol., 105,* 13–37.

Sutton-Smith, B., Roberts, J. M. & Kozelka, R. M. (1963) Games involvement in adults. *J. Soc. Psychol., 60,* 1, 15–30.

Swades, H. (1958) Less work—less leisure. In E. Larrabee & R. Meyersohn (Eds.) *Mass leisure.* Glencoe: Free Press.

Tannenbaum, A. H. (1962) Adolescent attitudes toward academic brilliance. New York: Columbia University Teachers' Coll. Bur. Publ.

Tanner, J. M. (1964) *Physique of the olympic athlete.* London: Allen & Unwin.

Tattersfield, R. C. (1971) Competitive sport and personality development. PhD thesis. University of Durham.

Taylor, G. B. (1970) Quality in recreation. In T. L. Burton (Ed.) *Recreation research and planning.* London: Allen & Unwin.

Taylor, I. (1971a) Soccer consciousness and soccer hooliganism. In S. Cohen, *Images of Deviance.* Harmonsworth: Penguin 134–64.

Taylor, I. (1971b) Football mad: a speculative sociology of soccer hooliganism. In Dunning E. (Ed.). The sociology of Sport. London: Cassell.

Thomson, I. (1968) Games must be a part of a conscious effort to accelerate social change. *Times Educ. Suppl.* 13 December, 1340.

Thorpe, E. (1973) Community schools—towards a definition. Aberdeen: *Educ. in the North,* 10, 33–39.

Thrasher, F. M. (1936) *The gang.* Chicago: University Press.

Toogood, J. E. (1967) The selection of children for responsibility in the junior school. Unpublished Dip. Educ. Guidance Dissertation, University of Manchester.

Turner, R. H. (1964) *The social context of ambition.* San Francisco: Chandler.

Ulbrich, J. (1971) Individual variants of physical fitness in boys from the age of 11 up to maturity and their selection for sports activities. *Medicine Dello Sport, 2,* 118–136.

Walster, E., Aronson, V., Abrahams, D. & Rottman, L. (1966) The importance of physical attractiveness in dating behaviour. *J. Pers. Soc. Psychol., 4,* 508–516.

Warburton, F. & Kane, J. E. (1967) Personality related to sport and physical ability. In J. E. Kane & C. Murray, (Eds.) *Readings in physical education.* London, Physical Education Association.

Ward, E. & Hardman, K. (1973) The influence of values on the role perceptions of men physical education teachers. An investigation for the N. W. Counties Physical Education Association.

Ward, E., Hardman, K. & Almond, L. (1968) Investigation into patterns of participation in physical activity of 11 to 18 year old boys. *Res. in Phys. Educ., 3,* 18–25.

Watson, A. W. S. (1970) The physique of a secondary school rugger team. *Brit. J. Phys. Educ., 1,* 1, -4.

Welford, A. T. (1968) *Fundamentals of skill.* London: Methuen.

West, D. J. (1967) *The young offender.* Harmondsworth: Penguin.

Westwood, L. J. (1967–8) The role of the teacher II. *Educ. Res.,* 10, 21–37.

Westergaard, J. (1970) The rediscovery of the cash nexus. *Socialist Register.*

Westergaard, J. (1974) *Men and work in modern Britain*, D. Weir (Ed.) London: Fontana.

Whitehead, N. J. (1969) Physical education in men's colleges and boys' schools. M Ed thesis. University of Leicester.

Whitehead, N. (1976) In Whitehead, N. & Hendry, L. B. (1976).

Whitehead, N. & Hendry, L. B. (1976) *Teaching physical education in England: description and analysis.* London: Lepus.

Whitfield, R. C. (1971) *Disciplines of the curriculum.* London: McGraw-Hill.

Whiting, H. T. A. & Stembridge, D. E. (1965) Personality and the persistent non-swimmer. *Res Quart., 36,* 3, 348–356.

Wilensky, H. K. (1964) High culture and mass culture. *New Society,* 14 May, 8–11.

Wilson, B. (1962) The teacher's role: a sociological analysis. *Br. J. Sociol., 13.*

Wilson, B. (1966) An approach to delinquency, *New Society,* February 3.

Wiseman, S. (1964) *Education and environment.* Manchester: University Press.

Witkin, H. A. (1965) Psychological differentiation and forms of pathology. *J. Abnorm. Psychol., 70,* 317–336.

Witkin, H. A., Dyk, R. B., Paterson, D. R. & Karp, S. A. (1962) *Psychological differentiation.* New York: Wiley.

Wolfle, D. (1961) National resources of ability. In Halsey, A. H. (Ed.) *Ability and educational opportunity.* Paris, O.E.C.D.

Wooller, K. (1975) The competitive factor. *Br. J. Phys. Ed., 6,* 4.

Yablonsky, L. (1967) *The violent gang.* Harmondsworth: Pelican.

Young, M. F. D. (1971) *Knowledge and control.* London: Collier-MacMillan.

Youth Service Development Council (1969) *Youth and community work in the 70s.* London: H.M.S.O.

INDEX

Index